Math Mammoth Grade 1 Skills Review Workbook

By Maria Miller

ISBN 978-1-942715-33-7

2017 EDITION

Contents

Chapter 3: Place Value Within 0-100

Chapter 4: Addition and Subtraction Facts

Chapter 5: Time

Chapter 6: Shapes and Measuring

Chapter 7: Adding and Subtracting Within 0-100

Chapter 8: Coins

Foreword

Math Mammoth Grade 1 Skills Review Workbook has been created to complement the lessons in the *Math Mammoth Grade 1* complete curriculum. It gives the students practice in reviewing what they have already studied, so the concepts and skills will become more established in their memory.

These review worksheets are designed to provide a spiral review of the concepts in the curriculum. This means that after a concept or skill has been studied in the main curriculum, it is then reviewed repeatedly over time in several different worksheets of this book.

This book is divided into chapters, according to the corresponding chapters in the *Math Mammoth Grade 1* curriculum. You can choose exactly when to use the worksheets within the chapter, and how many of them to use. Not all students need all of these worksheets to help them keep their math skills fresh, so please vary the amount of worksheets you assign your student(s) according to their need.

Each worksheet is designed to be one page, and includes a variety of exercises in a fun way without becoming too long and tedious. We have created a spreadsheet document that lists the lessons spiraled in each worksheet. This document is included with the digital (download) version. You can also download it at the following link:

https://www.mathmammoth.com/skills_review_workbooks/guides/Skills_Review_Grade1_Spiraling_Guide.xls

The printed answer key can be purchased separately or in the digital download version it is included in the zip file.

I wish you success in teaching math!

Maria Miller, the author

Skills Review 1

1. Write an addition sentence for each set of pictures.

2. Add. Then use the color code to color.

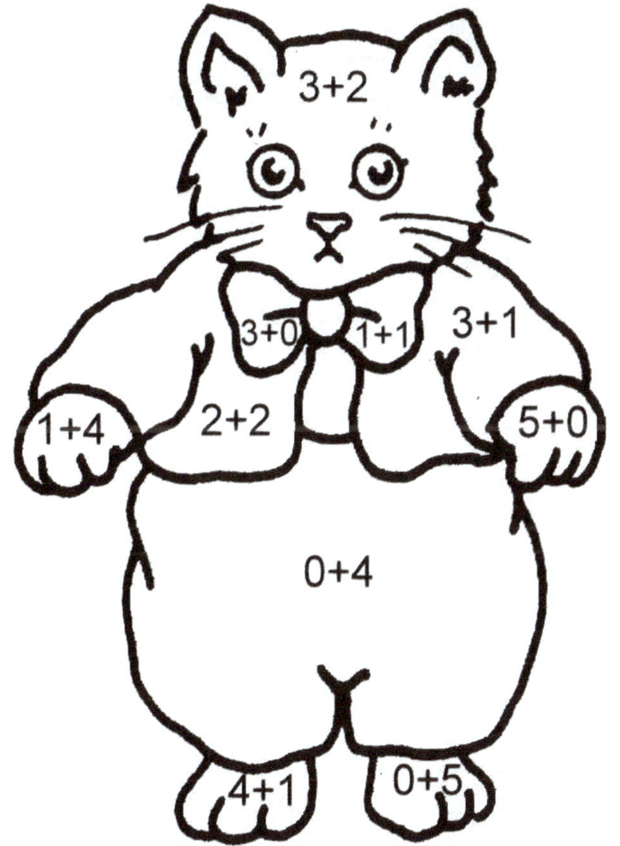

2 = red
3 = yellow
4 = blue
5 = orange

3. Circle the two groups that make up each number.

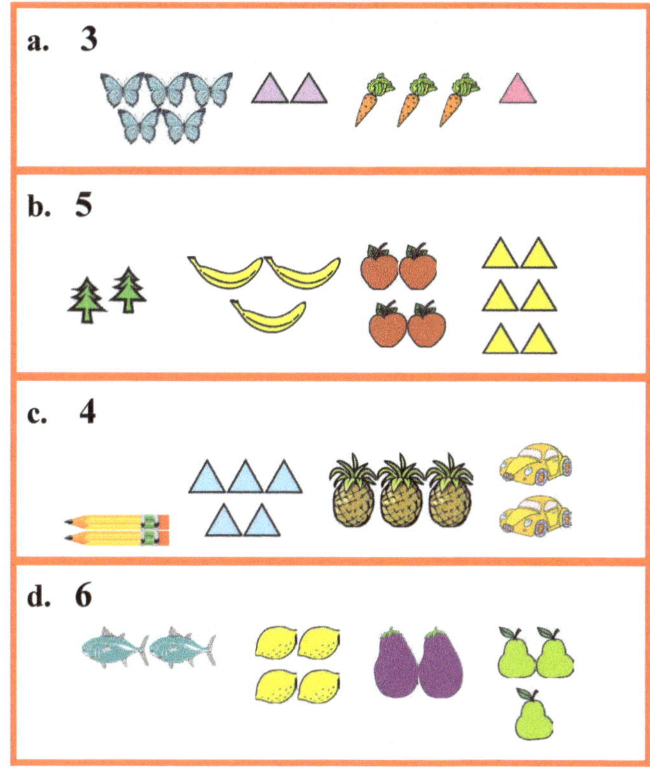

Skills Review 2

1. Which additions equal the number in the middle of the flower? Color them.

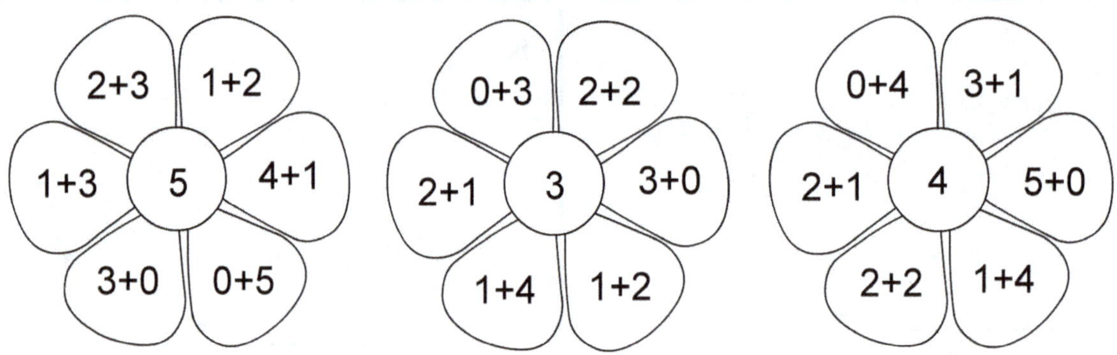

2. Write > or < .

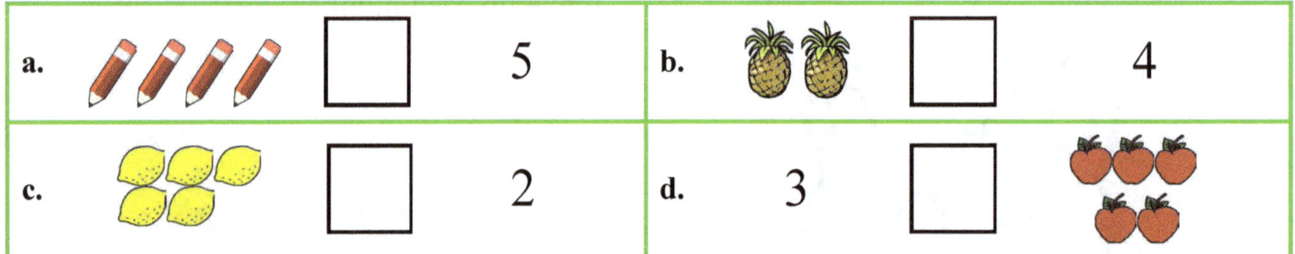

a.	☐	5	
b.	☐	4	
c.	☐	2	
d.	3	☐	

3. Draw pictures to illustrate the additions.

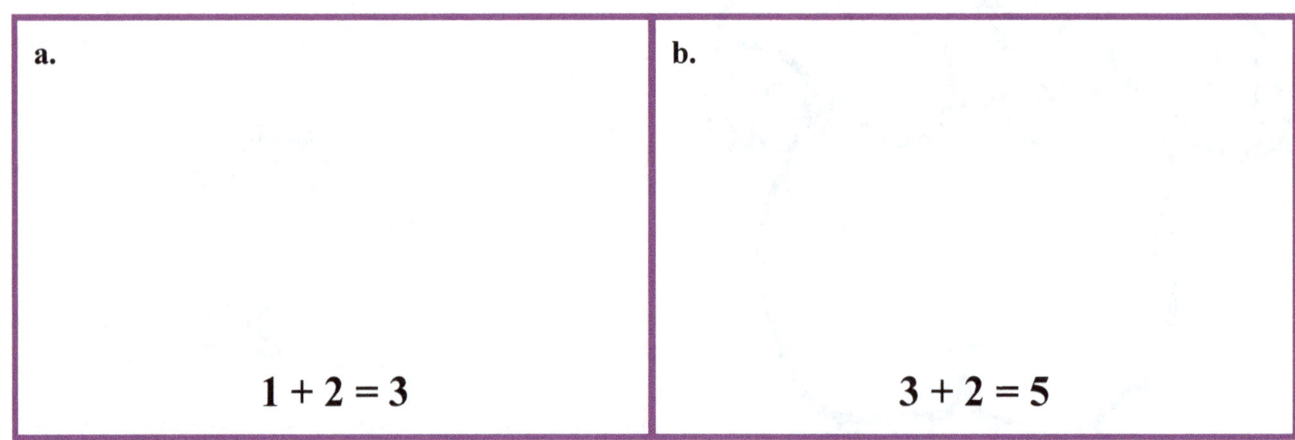

a.	b.
1 + 2 = 3	**3 + 2 = 5**

4. Practice adding in both orders.

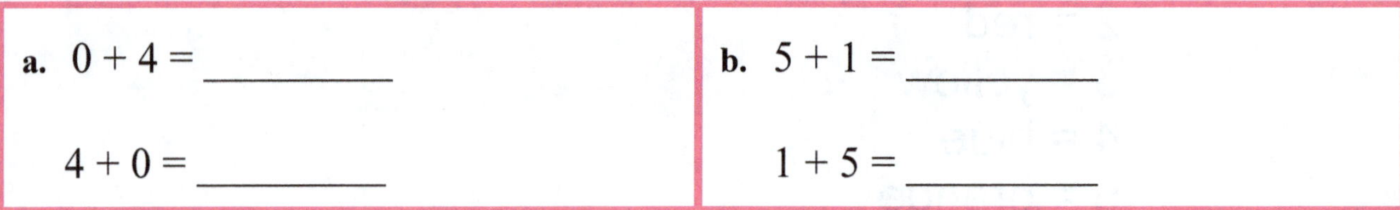

a.	b.
$0 + 4 =$ ________	$5 + 1 =$ ________
$4 + 0 =$ ________	$1 + 5 =$ ________

Skills Review 3

1. Count the objects and write the numbers on the correct lines.

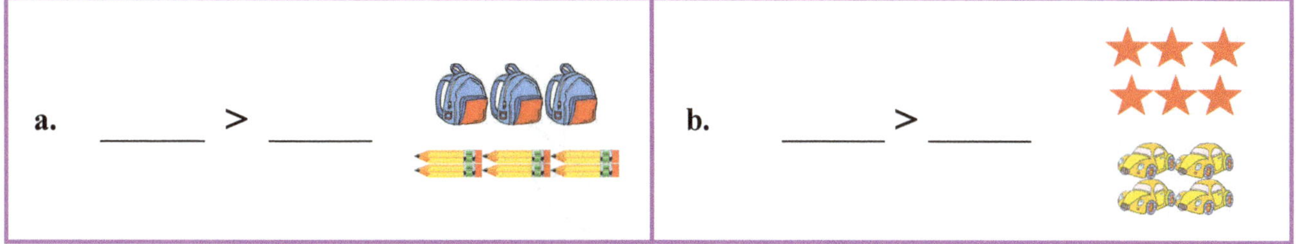

a. ______ > ______	**b.** ______ > ______

2. Write the missing numbers in the shapes.

a. 3 + ☐ = 5	**b.** 2 + 1 = ☐	**c.** ☐ + 3 = 4

3. Color the flower petals using the color guide. Then color the rest of the picture!

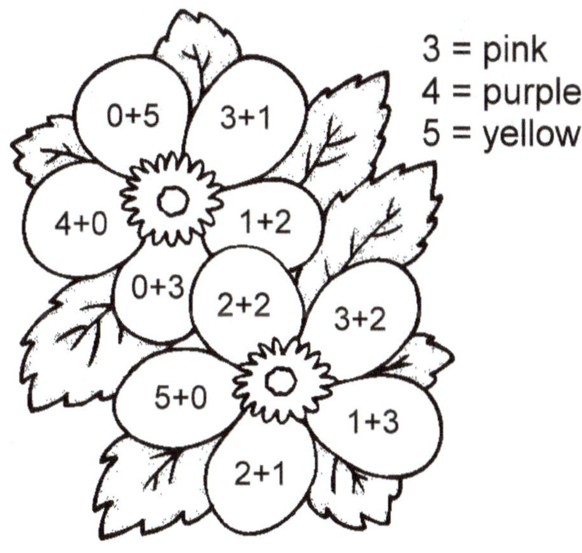

4. Circle the addition problem that equals the number.

a. 4	**b.** 2
0 + 5 2 + 3 1 + 3 3 + 3	1 + 1 3 + 0 0 + 4 1 + 3
c. 5	**d.** 3
4 + 2 5 + 0 3 + 4 1 + 3	1 + 2 4 + 1 1 + 1 2 + 0

Skills Review 4

1. Read the addition sentences and then color following the color code.

2. Fill in the missing numbers and complete the patterns!

a.	b.	c.
0 + ________ = 1	________ + 1 = 2	2 + 2 = ________
0 + ________ = 2	________ + 2 = 3	2 + 3 = ________
0 + ________ = 3	________ + 3 = 4	2 + 4 = ________
0 + ________ = 4	________ + 4 = 5	2 + 5 = ________
0 + ________ = 5	________ + 5 = 6	2 + 6 = ________

3. Write < or > between the two numbers.

a. 7 ☐ 4 **b.** 3 ☐ 5 **c.** 2 ☐ 3 **d.** 8 ☐ 6

Skills Review 5

1. Solve the additions in your head. If the sum is 5, color it with a green crayon. If the sum is 6, color it with a yellow crayon.

1 + 5	0 + 5	3 + 3	0 + 6
2 + 4	6 + 0	2 + 3	4 + 2
3 + 2	4 + 1	5 + 1	1 + 4

2. Draw more items to illustrate the missing number. Complete the addition sentence.

a.  __1__ + ______ = 4	**b.** 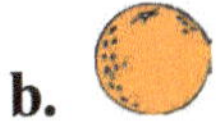 ______ + ______ = 3	**c.**  ______ + ______ = 6
d.  ______ + ______ = 5	**e.** ______ + ______ = 6	**f.**  ______ + ______ = 5

3. Which one is false? Circle it.

a. $4 > 5$ $1 < 3$	**b.** $3 > 2$ $4 < 3$	**c.** $2 < 0$ $5 > 3$

4. Add.

a. 4 + 2 = ______	**b.** 2 + 3 = ______	**c.** 1 + 1 = ______
2 + 2 = ______	1 + 3 = ______	0 + 5 = ______
3 + 2 = ______	0 + 3 = ______	1 + 4 = ______
1 + 2 = ______	3 + 3 = ______	6 + 0 = ______

Skills Review 6

1. Circle two numbers with a red crayon if they make 5. Circle two numbers with a blue crayon if they make 6. Note: Each number can only be circled once.

4	2	2	0	2	3
3	2	0	6	3	3
2	1	2	1	4	2
3	4	2	3	3	2
3	2	5	0	3	3

2. Draw the jumps to illustrate the addition and find the answer. You can use a different color for each number when you draw the jumps.

a. 5 + 4 = _______

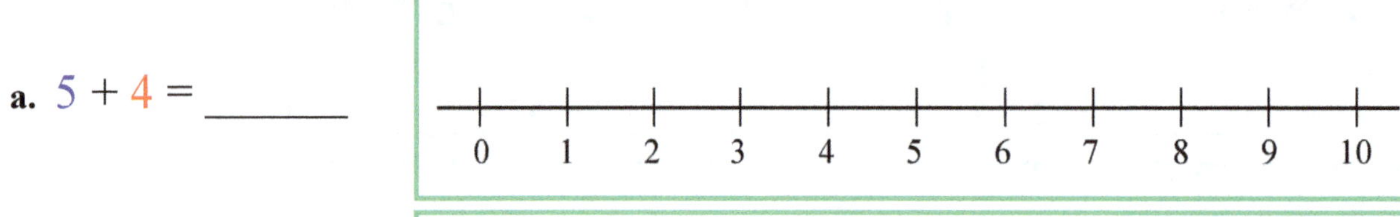

b. 6 + 3 = _______

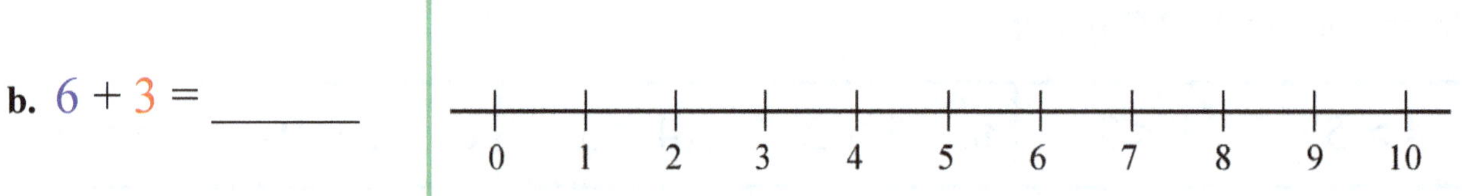

3. Add in your head. Then use the color code to color the picture.

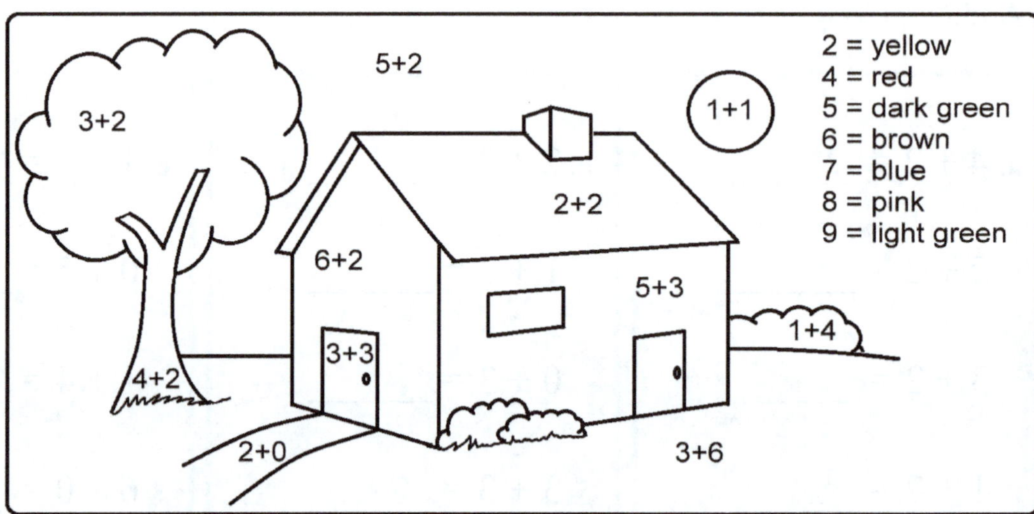

Skills Review 7

1. Add in your head. If the sum is 5, color it orange. If the sum is 6, color it yellow. If the sum is 7, color it light green.

$0 + 5$	$2 + 3$	$3 + 3$	$0 + 6$
$2 + 4$	$5 + 2$	$6 + 1$	$7 + 0$
$3 + 4$	$4 + 2$	$4 + 3$	$1 + 4$

2. Draw arrows (or jumps) to show the addition.

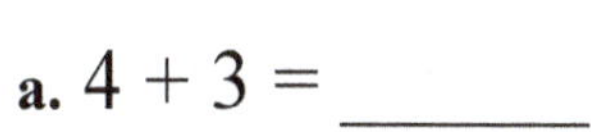

a. $4 + 3 =$ ______

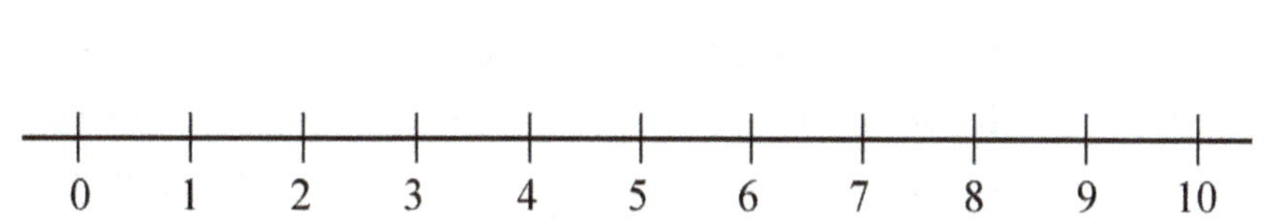

b. $5 + 1 =$ ______

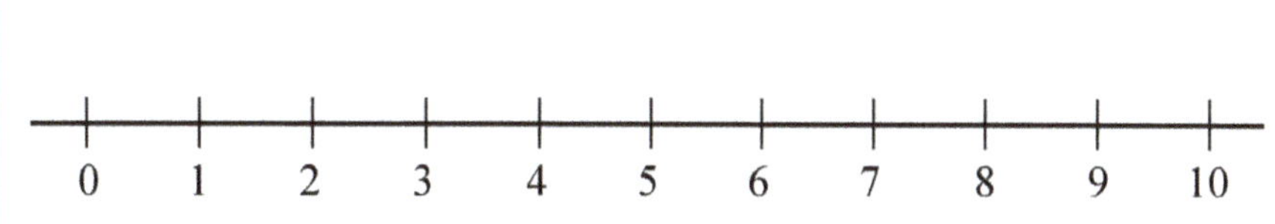

3. Add. Remember to write the answer *under* the line.

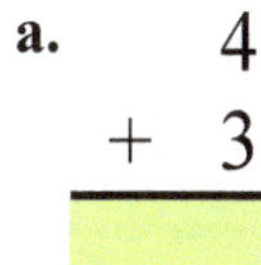

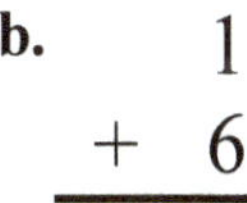

a. $4 + 3$

b. $1 + 6$

c. $5 + 2$

d. $1 + 3$

e. $6 + 0$

4. Solve the word problems. Draw pictures to help you!
Think: Are you asked the total? Or do you already know the total?

a. Mom baked three pies. Then, she baked four more. How many pies did Mom bake?

b. There are six animals in the yard. Four of them are dogs. How many are not dogs?

Skills Review 8

1. Add.

a.	b.	c.	d.	e.
4	6	3	7	2
+ 4	+ 2	+ 4	+ 1	+ 4

2. Solve the word problems. Draw pictures to help you!
Think: Are you asked the total? Or do you already know the total?

a. Laura picked five pink flowers and three red flowers. How many flowers did Laura pick?

b. Mary needs six buttons. She found four buttons in a box. How many more buttons does Mary need?

3. Fill in the missing numbers. Notice the patterns!

a.	b.	c.
2 + ______ = 8	1 + ______ = 7	5 + ______ = 6
3 + ______ = 8	2 + ______ = 7	4 + ______ = 6
4 + ______ = 8	3 + ______ = 7	3 + ______ = 6
5 + ______ = 8	4 + ______ = 7	2 + ______ = 6

4. Write >, <, or = in the box.

a. 8 ☐ 8 **b.** 4 ☐ 6 **c.** 8 ☐ 7 **d.** 7 ☐ 5

Skills Review 9

1. Circle **three** numbers with a red crayon if they make 7. Circle three numbers with a blue crayon if they make 8. Note: Each number can only be circled once.

4	2	5	2	2	3
3	2	0	2	3	3
0	1	2	1	4	2
2	4	2	3	3	2
3	5	0	2	3	3

2. Add.

a. $2 + 7 = $ ___

b. $3 + 4 = $ ___

c. $5 + 4 = $ ___

d. $4 + 2 = $ ___

e. $6 + 3 = $ ___

3. Solve. You can draw pictures to help.

a. Amy found 5 pretty shells at the beach. Lola found 3 pretty shells. How many pretty shells did the girls find?

b. Mom made 9 sandwiches. Two were peanut butter and jelly, 3 were tuna, and the rest were cheese. How many cheese sandwiches did Mom make?

c. Josh has 2 cats. Bonnie has 3 dogs. Carol has 2 rabbits. How many pets do the children have in total?

Skills Review 10

1. Solve the word problem. You can draw a picture to help you!

There were 8 cookies. Alan ate 3, David ate 2, and Emma ate the rest.

How many cookies did Emma eat?

2. Which additions equal the number in the middle of the flower? Color them.

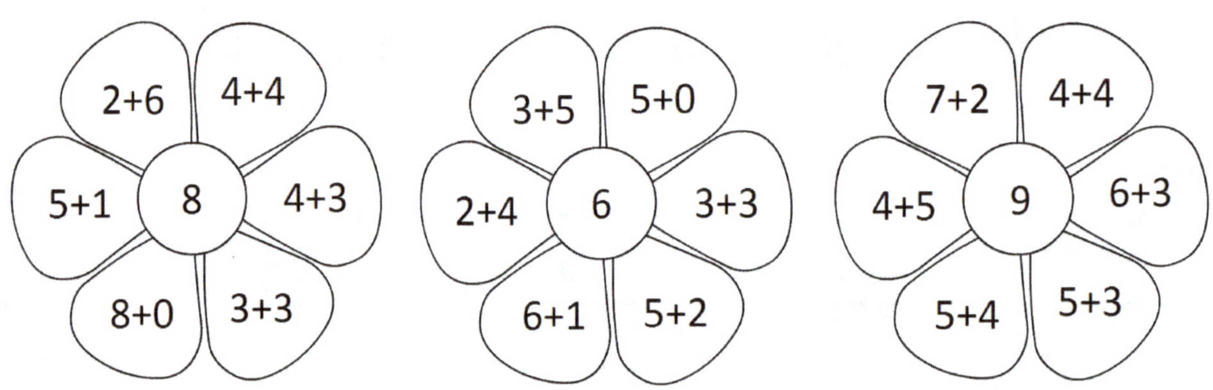

3. Draw arrows (or jumps) to show the addition. Use a different color to draw the jumps for each number.

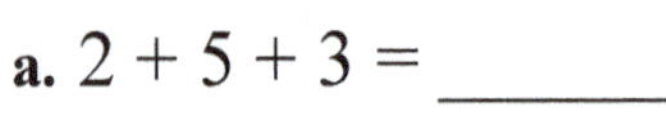

a. 2 + 5 + 3 = ______

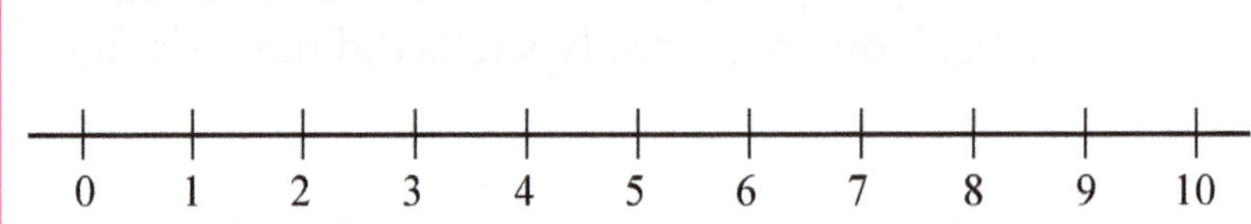

b. 1 + 3 + 4 = ______

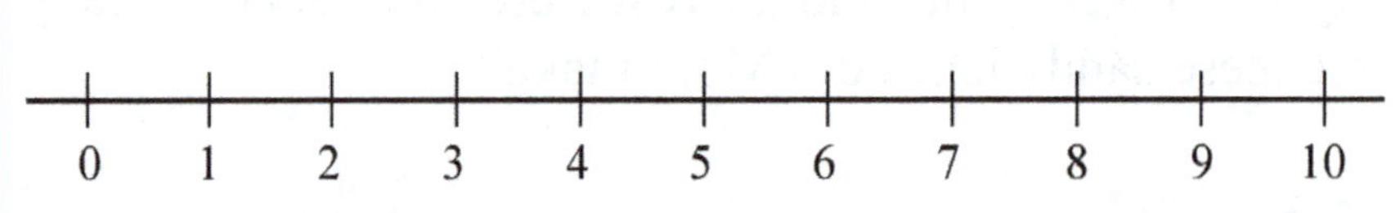

4. Add in your head. Compare the sum to the other number. Write >, <, or = in the box.

a. 3 + 4 ☐ 8 **b.** 1 + 5 ☐ 6 **c.** 5 + 3 ☐ 7 **d.** 2 + 6 ☐ 5

Skills Review 11

1. Choose the number from the numbers at the top of the box that makes the sentence true.

0 5 3 2 > ______	4 9 2 7 < ______	6 1 5 4 > ______
1 3 6 4 < ______	2 8 10 5 > ______	7 4 9 8 < ______

2. Fill in the missing numbers in the addition puzzle.

4	+		=	9
+				
	+	2	=	5
=		+		+
7				
		=		=
	+	6	=	8

3. Add. You can add in any order.

a.	**b.**	**c.**	**d.**	**e.**
2	0	6	7	4
7	2	1	1	0
+ 3	+ 5	+ 2	+ 1	+ 3

Skills Review 12

1. Challenges! First add in your head. Then write <, > or = .

a. 5 + 4 ☐ 7 + 3   **b.** 4 + 1 ☐ 2 + 3   **c.** 8 ☐ 2 + 5

2. Write the missing numbers. Notice the patterns!

a.	b.	c.
9 + ______ = 10	5 + ______ = 9	1 + ______ = 8
8 + ______ = 10	4 + ______ = 9	2 + ______ = 8
7 + ______ = 10	3 + ______ = 9	3 + ______ = 8
6 + ______ = 10	2 + ______ = 9	4 + ______ = 8

3. Solve the word problems.

a. Marty has 8 pencils, but he can only find 5.
How many pencils are missing?

b. Kendra put 3 gray kittens, 6 black kittens, and 1 orange kitten into a basket. How many kittens are in the basket?

Skills Review 13

1. Add. You can add in any order.

a.	b.	c.	d.	e.
3	5	4	6	0
0	1	0	2	3
+ 6	+ 2	+ 1	+ 1	+ 4

2. Write a subtraction sentence to match the picture.

a.

___ − ___ = ____

b.

___ − ___ = ____

c.

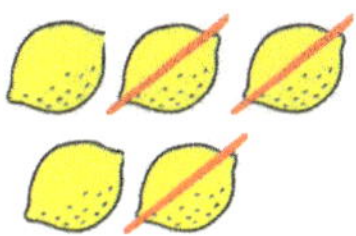

___ − ___ = ____

d

___ − ___ = ____

e.

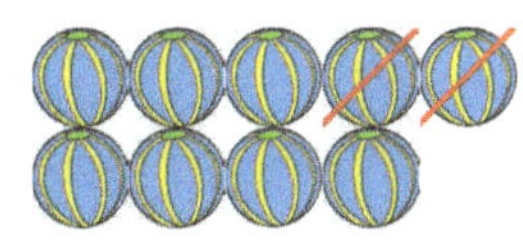

___ − ___ = ____

f.

___ − ___ = ____

3. Write the missing numbers.

a. 3 + ____ = 9	**b.** 4 + 4 = ____	**c.** ____ + 6 = 10
d. 5 + ____ = 7	**e.** ____ + 3 = 8	**f.** 9 + 0 = ____

Skills Review 14

1. Draw steps (or a single arrow) to illustrate the subtraction sentence.

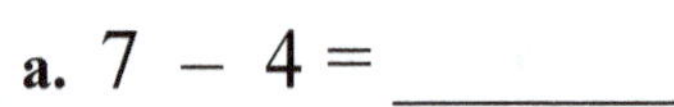

a. 7 – 4 = ________

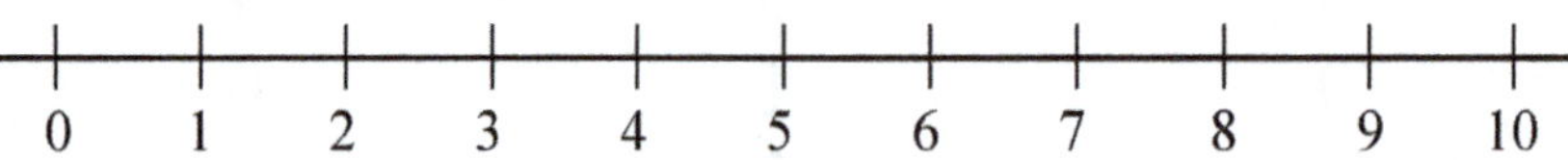

b. 6 – 2 = ________

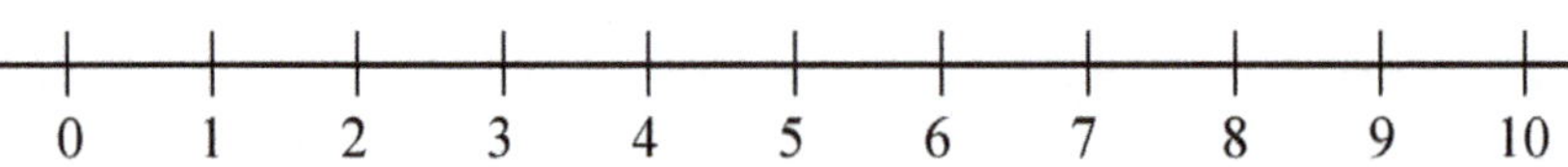

c. 9 – 3 = ________

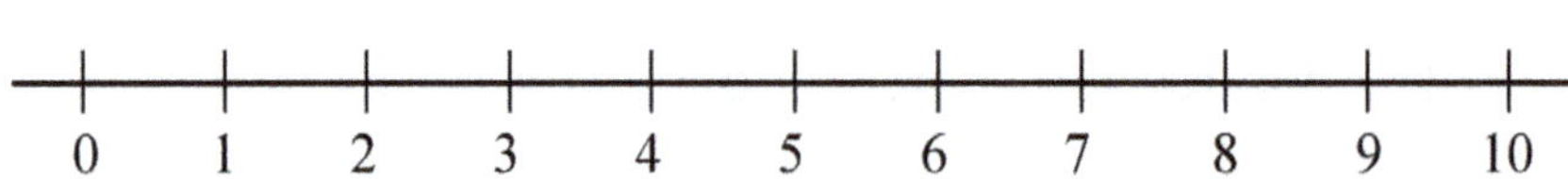

2. Draw small circles to illustrate the numbers and cross out some of them to match the subtraction problem.

a. 9 – 6 = ______	**b.** 5 – 5 = ______	**c.** 7 – 1 = ______
d. 6 – 4 = ______	**e.** 10 – 3 = ______	**f.** 8 – 2 = ______

3. Solve the word problems.

a. Mandy put 7 kittens into a basket. Five of them ran away.
How many kittens were left in the basket?

b. Eric has 6 grapes in a bowl and 4 grapes in his hand.
How many grapes does Eric have?

Skills Review 15

1. There were 7 pears on the table. Then some were taken away. Complete the subtraction and addition sentences for each picture.

a.	b.	c.

6 + ______ = 7	4 + ______ = 7	_____ + _____ = 7
7 – ______ = 6	7 – _____ = _____	7 – _____ = _____

2. Solve the problems in your head. Then write <, >, or = .

a. 8 ☐ 5 + 5   b. 7 – 3 ☐ 5   c. 3 + 4 ☐ 6 – 2

d. 9 – 1 ☐ 8 + 0   e. 6 – 4 ☐ 8 – 6   f. 10 – 4 ☐ 3 + 2

3. Todd has 3 goldfish, 4 cats, and 2 dogs.
   How many pets does Todd have?

4. Subtract 2 or 3. You can count down. Compare the problems.

a.	b.	c.	d.
8 – 2 = _____	5 – 2 = _____	9 – 2 = _____	6 – 2 = _____
8 – 3 = _____	5 – 3 = _____	9 – 3 = _____	6 – 3 = _____

Skills Review 16

1. Look at the subtraction problems. If you can take away that many, color it.

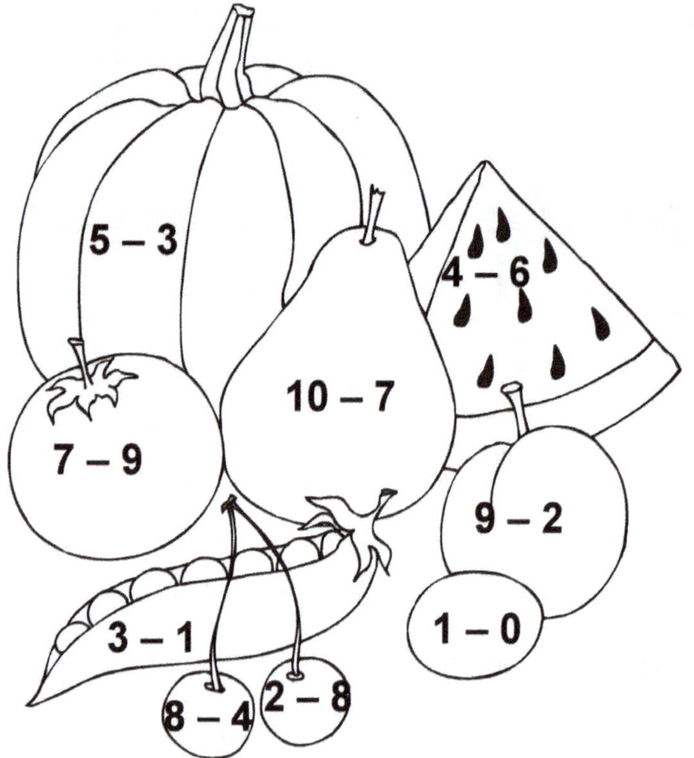

2. Continue the pattern as long as you can!

7 – 0 = ____

7 – 1 = ____

7 – 2 = ____

7 – ____ = ____

____ – ____ = ____

____ – ____ = ____

____ – ____ = ____

____ – ____ = ____

3. Subtract. Remember to write the answer below the line!

a.	b.	c.	d.	e.
9	10	7	5	6
– 4	– 7	– 7	– 0	– 1

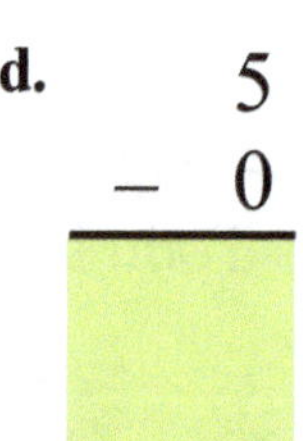

4. Make an addition sentence and a subtraction sentence from the same picture.

a.	b.
____ + ____ = ____	____ + ____ = ____
____ – ____ = ____	____ – ____ = ____

Skills Review 17

1. Draw an arrow for the subtraction sentence and solve.

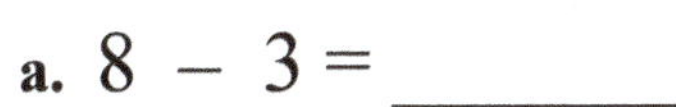

a. 8 – 3 = ________

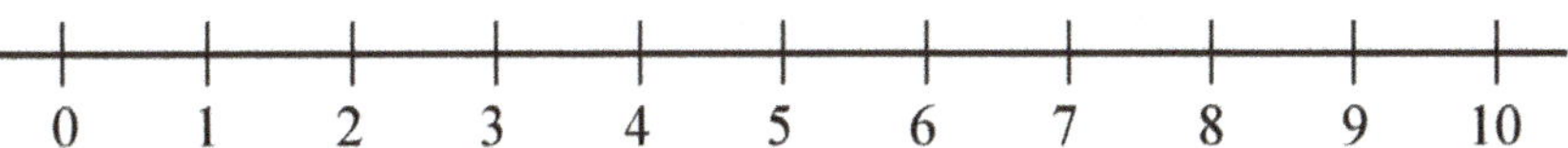

b. 6 – 5 = ________

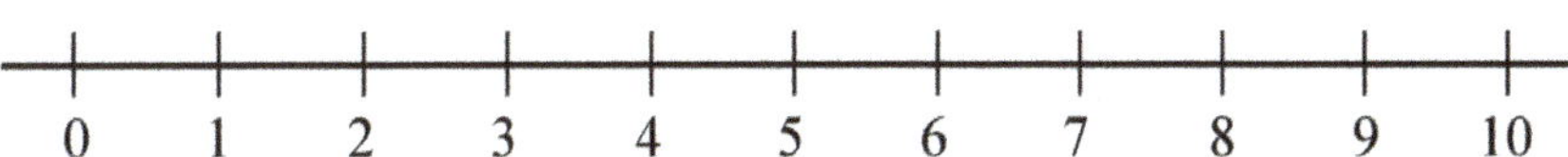

2. Write one addition and two subtraction sentences.

a. 2 + 3 = 5

5 – ______ = ______

or 5 – ______ = ______

b. ______ + ______ = ______

______ – ______ = ______

or ______ – ______ = ______

3. Is the subtraction true or false? If it is false, color the balloon.

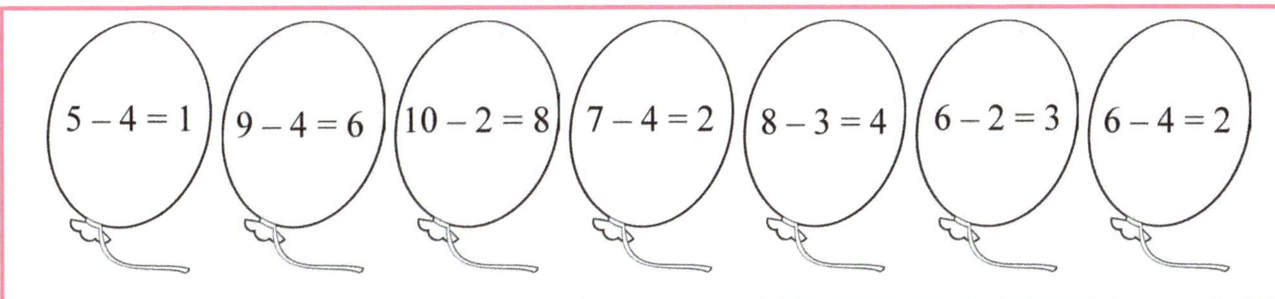

4. Subtract.

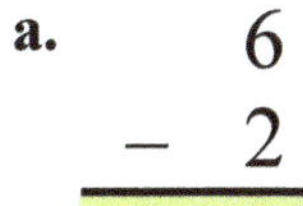

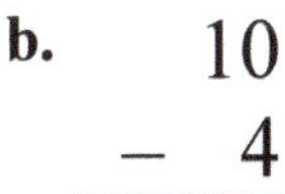

a. 6 − 2

b. 10 − 4

c. 9 − 0

d. 7 − 5

e. 5 − 1

Skills Review 18

1. Color the objects using the color guide. Write 1 addition and 2 subtraction problems.

6 green apples 4 red apples

a. ______ + ______ = ______

______ − ______ = ______

or ______ − ______ = ______

5 orange fish 1 blue fish

b. ______ + ______ = ______

______ − ______ = ______

or ______ − ______ = ______

2. Draw circles to match the missing number in the addition.
   Write the missing number on the line.

a.  3 + 2 + ______ = 8	**b.**  ______ + 1 + 5 = 10	**c.** 4 + ______ + 2 = 9

3. Solve the word problems. Write an addition and a subtraction sentence for each problem.

a. Katie has 8 dolls. Five of them have black hair and the rest have red hair. How many dolls have red hair?

______ + ______ = ______

______ − ______ = ______

b. There were 10 eggs in a carton. Three of them fell out and broke. How many eggs were left in the carton?

______ + ______ = ______

______ − ______ = ______

Skills Review 19

1. Write the fact families.

a. Numbers: 8, 2, _____	b. Numbers: 6, 3, _____
_____ + _____ = _____	_____ + _____ = _____
_____ + _____ = _____	_____ + _____ = _____
_____ – _____ = _____	_____ – _____ = _____
_____ – _____ = _____	_____ – _____ = _____

2. Complete the subtraction puzzle.

9	–	5	=	
–				
	–	2	=	4
=		–		–
3				
		=		=
	–	2	=	3

3. Solve the word problems

a. Andy picked 5 oranges, Ellie picked 3 oranges, and Ben picked 2 oranges. How many oranges did they pick in total?

b. Amy had 8 pencils. Then, she gave 4 pencils to a friend. How many pencils did she have left?

Skills Review 20

1. Carl has 4 balloons and Alan has 3 more balloons than Carl.

a. Draw the balloons that Carl and Alan have.

Carl:

Alan:

b. How many balloons does Alan have? _______ balloons.

c. Make a problem about Carl's and Alan's balloons. You can write it here or tell your teacher.

2. Draw circles and write two *different* fact families for which the sum is 9.

a. 9 /	**b.** 9 /
______ + ______ = ______	______ + ______ = ______
______ + ______ = ______	______ + ______ = ______
______ – ______ = ______	______ – ______ = ______
______ – ______ = ______	______ – ______ = ______

3. Write the missing numbers.

a. 5 + _____ + 3 = 10	**b.** 7 – _____ = 3	**c.** _____ + 4 = 4

Skills Review 21

1. Solve the difference between the numbers. Then write an addition. Be careful.

a. from 4 to 9	**b.** from 3 to 7	**c.** from 6 to 8
______ steps	______ steps	______ steps
4 + ______ = 9	3 + ______ = 7	6 + ______ = 8

2. Each flower contains the numbers for *two* sums (such as 2 + 3 = 5 and 7 + 1 = 8). Using a different color for each sum, color the flower petals.

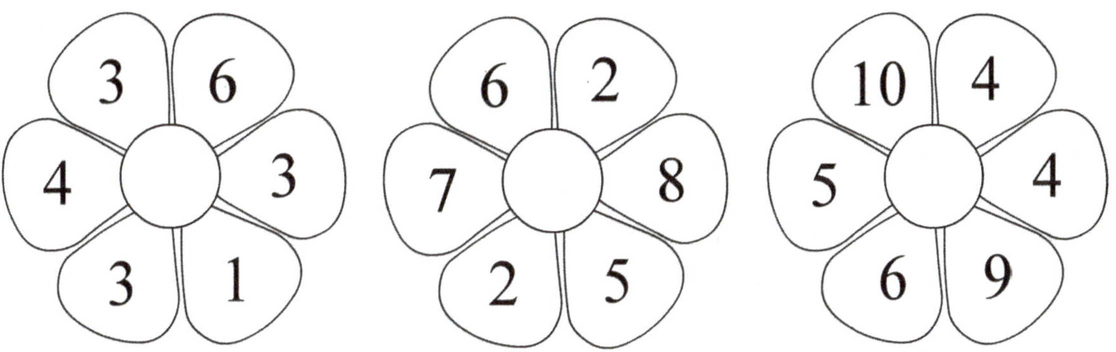

3. Solve the problems. Think carefully: Is it asking for the <u>total</u>? OR is it asking, "How many <u>more</u>?"

a. There are 7 turtles swimming in the pond and 3 turtles sitting in the grass.

How many turtles are there together?

There are how many more turtles swimming in the pond than the turtles sitting in the grass?

b. Eddie is 10 years old and his brother Dan is 3 years old.
How much older is Eddie than Dan?

Skills Review 22

1. Write the missing numbers.

a. _____ + 8 + 2 = 10	**b.** 9 – _____ = 4	**c.** _____ + 4 = 8

2. Write a subtraction problem to match the number line jumps.

a. _____ – _____ = _____

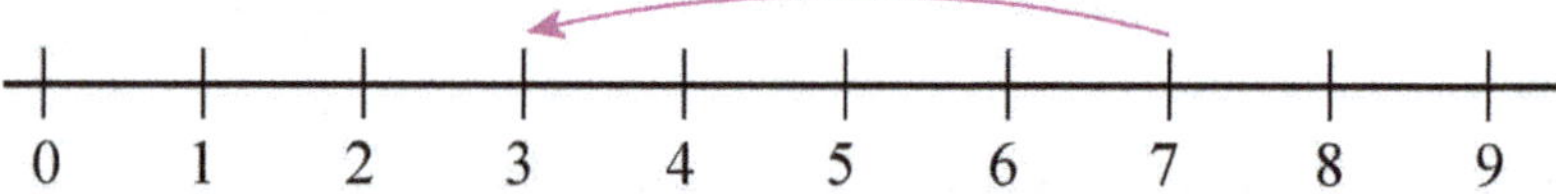

b. _____ – _____ = _____

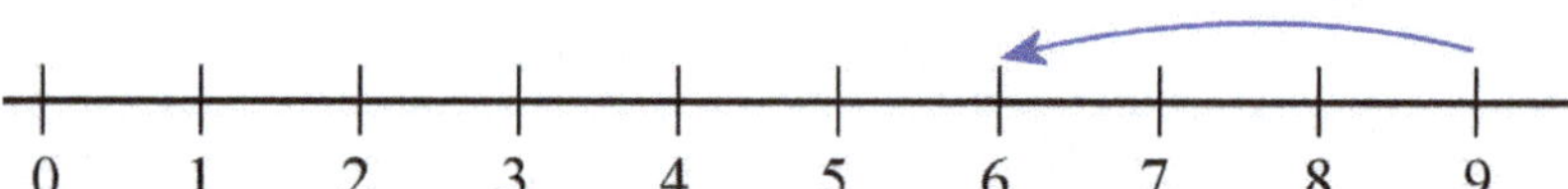

3. Solve the problems.

a. Alex has 9 crayons. Megan has 7 crayons. How many fewer crayons does Megan have than Alex?
b. Cathy has 3 red balloons, 2 green balloons, and 2 orange balloons. How many balloons does Cathy have in total?

4. Write a subtraction problem, using the same numbers, under each "how many more" problem. Solve the subtraction problem *first*.

a. 3 + _____ = 9	**b.** 5 + _____ = 7	**c.** 5 + _____ = 10
_____ – _____ = _____	_____ – _____ = _____	_____ – _____ = _____

Skills Review 23

1. Write the missing numbers.

a. ______ − 5 = 5	**b.** 3 + 4 + 2 = _____	**c.** 2 + ______ = 8

2. Draw more. Solve.

		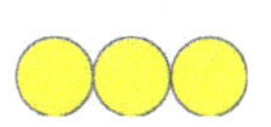
a. ______ + 4 = 9	**b.** ______ + 8 = 10	**c.** ______ + 3 = 6

3. Draw a line from each number to its name.

17	eighteen
13	sixteen
19	fourteen
16	seventeen
18	nineteen
14	thirteen

4. Name and write the numbers.

a. 6 tens 3 ones ______________________ _______

b. 4 tens 7 ones ______________________ _______

c. 2 tens 5 ones ______________________ _______

d. 7 tens 0 ones ______________________ _______

Skills Review 24

1. Break the numbers into tens and ones.

a.	b.	c.
57 = _____ + _____	39 = _____ + _____	82 = _____ + _____
d.	**e.**	**f.**
61 = _____ + _____	23 = _____ + _____	78 = _____ + _____

2. Fill in the missing items.

a. 10 + _____ = _____ _____*fifteen*_____

b. 10 + _____ = 19 _____________

c. 10 + 3 = _____ _____________

d. 10 + _____ = 17 _____________

3. Subtract. Do not write the answers; just solve them in your head.
Then compare, and write < , > , or = .

a. 8 ☐ 9 – 1 **b.** 10 – 5 ☐ 4 **c.** 9 – 6 ☐ 10 – 5

4. Solve the problems.

Matt has 3 books and Sarah has 7 books.

How many books do they have in total?

How many more books does Sarah have than Matt?

Skills Review 25

1. Write the missing numbers.

15 _______ 17 _______ _______ 20 21 _______ _______ _______ 25

_______ 74 75 _______ 77 _______ _______ _______ _______ 82

2. Add or subtract in your head. Then color using the color guide.

20 = green

30 = purple

50 = yellow

60 = pink

90 = gray

100 = brown

3. Solve the problems.

a. Tammy needs 6 sheets of paper to do a craft project, but she can only find 3. How many more sheets of paper does Tammy need?

b. Andrew was watching cars go by his house. He saw 2 blue cars, 4 red cars, and 1 black car. How many cars did Andrew see?

Skills Review 26

1. Fill in the missing numbers.

a. 70 + ☐ = 100	**b.** ☐ – 20 = 60	**c.** 70 – ☐ = 30
d. ☐ + 10 = 50	**e.** 90 – ☐ = 40	**f.** 80 + ☐ = 80

2. Write < , > or = .

a. 70 + 4 ☐ 60 + 7 **b.** 20 + 8 ☐ 8 + 20

c. 40 + 2 ☐ 30 + 5 **d.** 60 + 3 ☐ 90 + 9

3. Solve the problems.

a. Adam has 5 dollars and he wants to buy a book that costs 9 dollars. How much more money does he need to buy the book?

b. Carly baked 7 cupcakes. Then her brother ate 3 of them. How many cupcakes does Carly have left?

4.

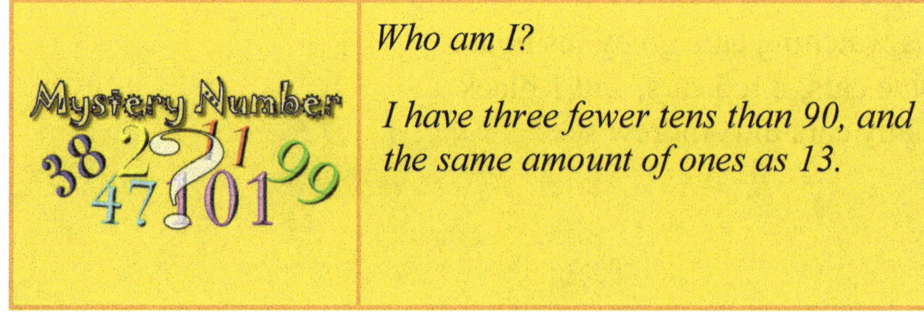

Who am I?

I have three fewer tens than 90, and the same amount of ones as 13.

Skills Review 27

1. Put the numbers in order from the smallest to the largest.

a. 53, 87, 39 _____ < _____ < _____	**b.** 25, 19, 13 _____ < _____ < _____
c. 37, 56, 60 _____ < _____ < _____	**d.** 33, 52, 27 _____ < _____ < _____

2. Write the number that is...

a.	**b.**	**c.**
one more than 115 ______	two more than 121 ______	ten more than 130 ______
one less than 110 ______	two less than 103 ______	ten less than 145 ______

3. Which additions and subtractions equal the number in the middle of the flower? Color them.

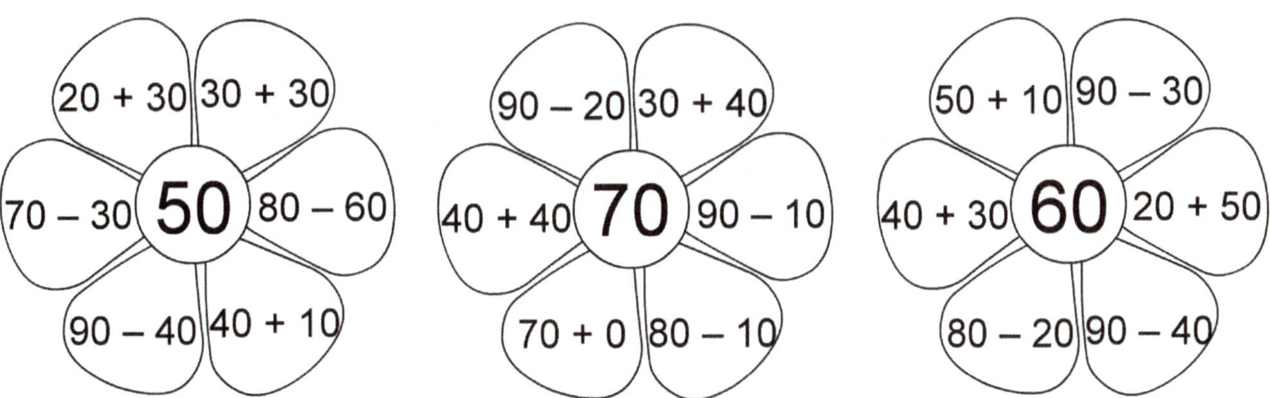

4. There were 10 cherries in a bowl. Rick ate 3 cherries, Carol ate 5 cherries, and Sam ate the rest. How many cherries did Sam eat?

Skills Review 28

1. Fill in the table.

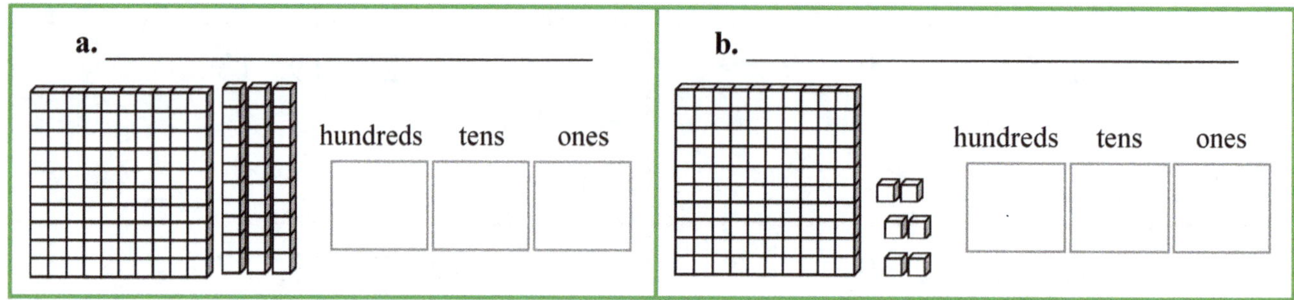

2. Continue the skip-counting patterns.

a. 12, 17, ______, ______, ______, ______, ______, ______

b. 24, 27, ______, ______, ______, ______, ______, ______

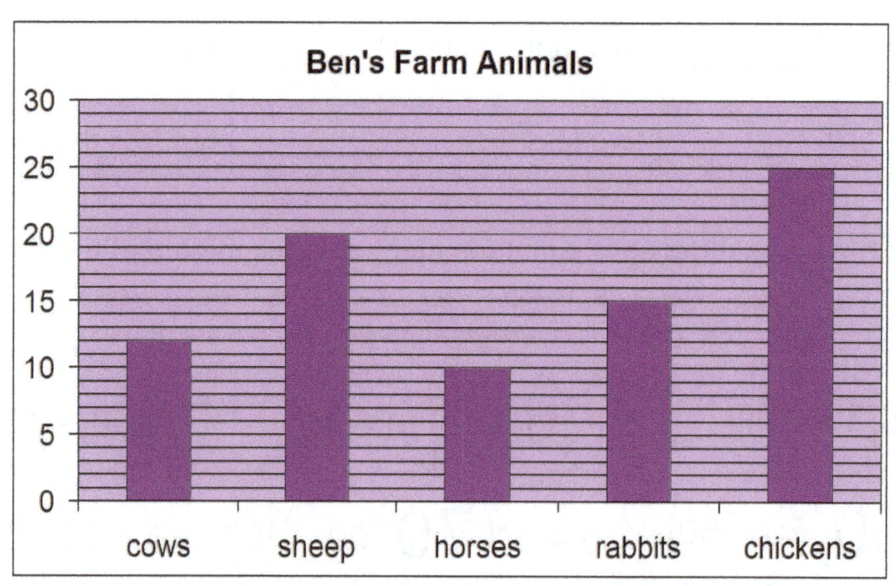

3. **a.** How many sheep does Ben have? ________ And rabbits? ________

b. Ben has more ____________________ than any other animal.

c. Ben has fewer ____________________ than any other animal.

d. How many more cows than horses does Ben have? _______ cows

Skills Review 29

1. Count the pieces of fruit. Use tally marks to keep track.

	Tally Marks	Count
Apples		
Pears		
Oranges		

2. Fill in the missing numbers. This chart starts at 93 and ends at 122.

93	94			97	98		100		
103			106			109			
		115			118			121	122

3. The bar graph shows foods that people ordered at a restaurant on a Friday.

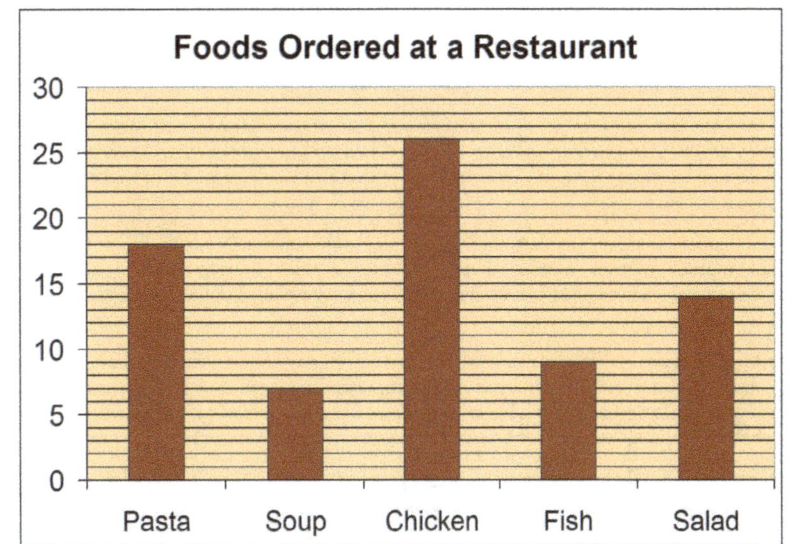

a. The food that was ordered the least was

_________________ .

b. The food that was ordered the most was

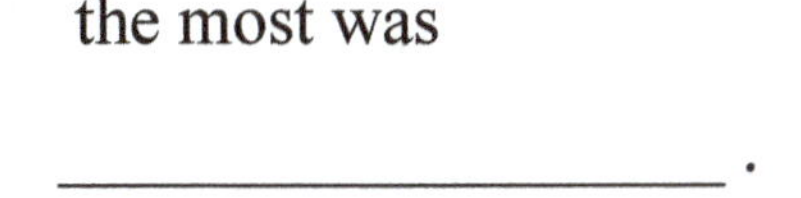

_________________ .

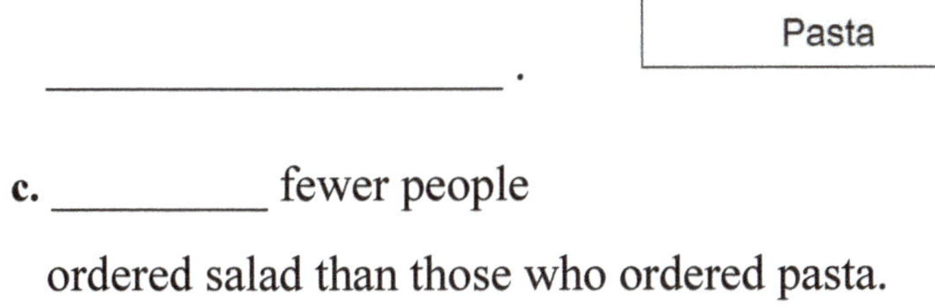

c. _________ fewer people ordered salad than those who ordered pasta.

Skills Review 30

1. Do the tally marks match the bar graph? If not, correct the tally.

	Tally Marks
Balls	𝍸 𝍸 𝍷𝍷
Cars	𝍸 𝍸 𝍸 𝍷𝍷𝍷𝍷
Dolls	𝍸 𝍸 𝍸 𝍸 𝍸 𝍷
Yo-yos	𝍸 𝍸

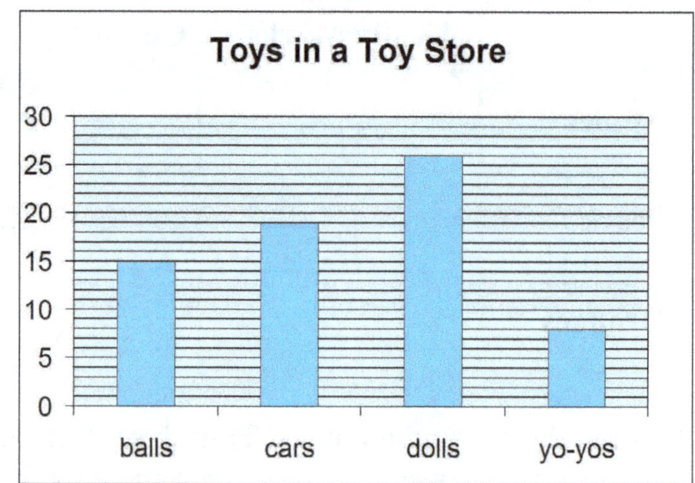

2. Circle two numbers with a red crayon if they make 4. Circle two numbers with a blue crayon if they make 5. Note: Each number can only be circled once.

4	2	2	0	2	3
3	2	0	4	3	2
2	1	2	1	4	2
3	4	2	3	3	2
3	2	5	0	3	3

3. Subtract.

a. $4 - 3 =$ ____ **b.** $5 - 0 =$ ____ **c.** $5 - 2 =$ ____ **d.** $4 - 1 =$ ____ **e.** $5 - 4 =$ ____ **f.** $4 - 2 =$ ____

4. Sarah is 9 years old and Mandy is 5 years old.
How much older is Sarah than Mandy?

Skills Review 31

1. Amy asked some people, "What is your favorite flavor of ice cream?"

   a. How many people did Amy ask? _______

   b. How many *more* people like chocolate chip than like strawberry? _______

   c. How many people like chocolate chip? _______

	Tally Marks
Vanilla	卌 卌 卌
Chocolate	卌 卌
Strawberry	卌 II
Chocolate chip	卌 卌 III

2. Continue the skip-counting patterns.

   a. 14, 24, 34, ________, ________, ________, ________, ________

   b. 15, 17, 19, ________, ________, ________, ________, ________

3. Continue the patterns!

a.	b.	c.
5 + _____ = 9	80 − _____ = 60	10 + _____ = 90
4 + _____ = 9	80 − _____ = 50	20 + _____ = 90
3 + _____ = 9	80 − _____ = 40	30 + _____ = 90
____ + _____ = 9	_____ − _____ = 30	_____ + _____ = 90
____ + _____ = 9	_____ − _____ = 20	_____ + _____ = 90

4. Carla picked 4 flowers, Karen picked 3 flowers, and Chloe picked 2 flowers. How many flowers did the girls pick in total?

Skills Review 32

1. Color the snail using the color guide.

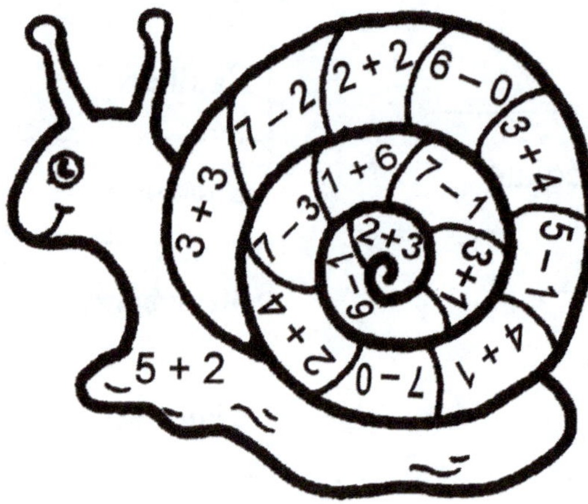

4 = blue
5 = green
6 = purple
7 = pink

2. Fill in the missing numbers.

a. _______ + 80 = 100	**b.** 64 – _______ = 54	**c.** 50 + _______ = 80
d. 60 – _______ = 30	**e.** _______ – 70 = 10	**f.** _______ + 10 = 35

3. The bar graph shows how many stickers some children have in their sticker collections.

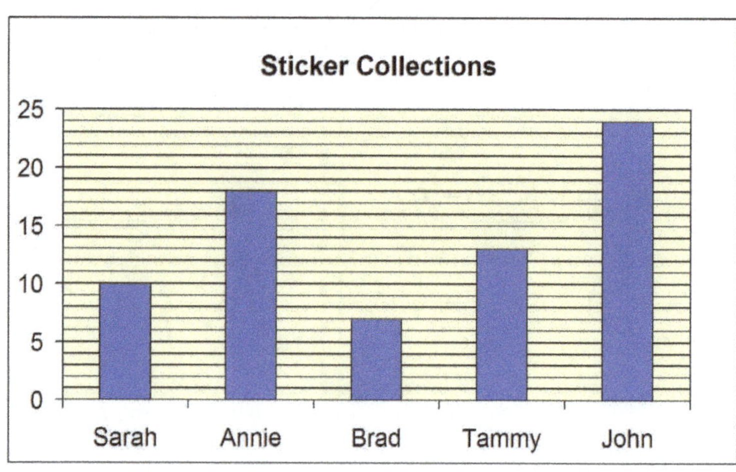

a. How many stickers do Sarah

and Brad have in total? _______

Make 2 more questions about the bar graph. You can write them here or tell them to your teacher.

b.

c.

Skills Review 33

1. Write a problem to match the number line jumps.

a. ______ − ______ = ______

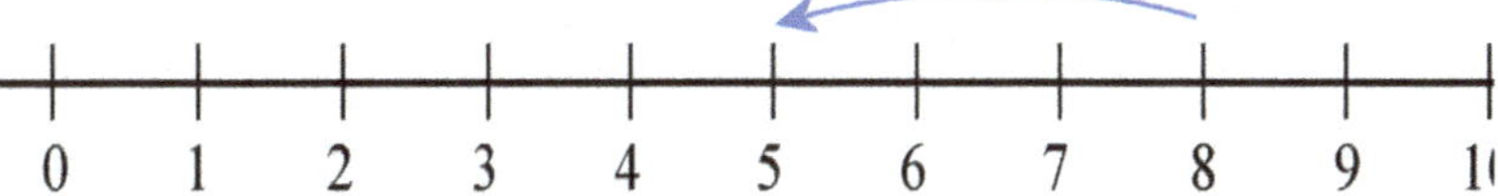

b. ______ + ______ = ______

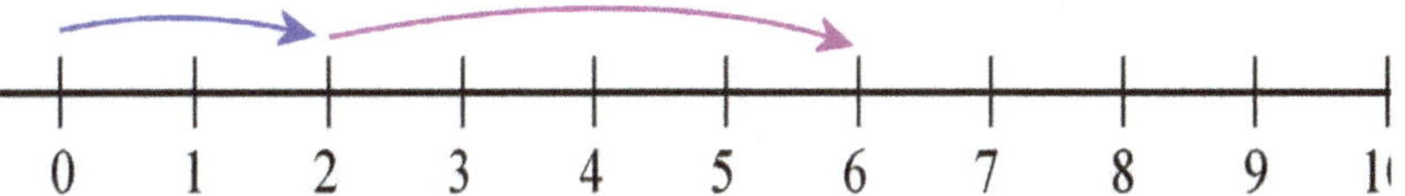

2. Complete the addition and subtraction puzzle.

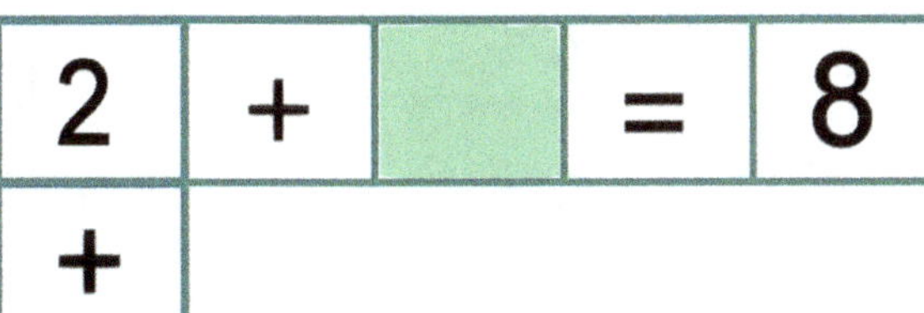

2	+		=	8
+				
	−	4	=	0
=		−		+
6		3		
		=		=
	−		=	7

3. Subtract.

a. $8 - 2 =$ ______

b. $6 - 4 =$ ______

c. $5 - 0 =$ ______

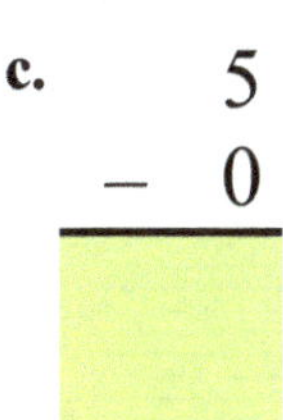

d. $7 - 5 =$ ______

e. $8 - 6 =$ ______

f. $6 - 5 =$ ______

4. Solve the problems.

a. Jerry's silly goat pulled 2 red shirts, 4 blue shirts, and 3 green shirts off of the clothesline. How many shirts got pulled off of the clothesline in total?

b. Eight little kittens were playing in the yard. Then 3 of them went into the barn. How many kittens were left in the yard?

Skills Review 34

1. Find ways through the maze so that the sum of the numbers is 9.
   Hint: Start with the 2 or 3 next to the arrow.

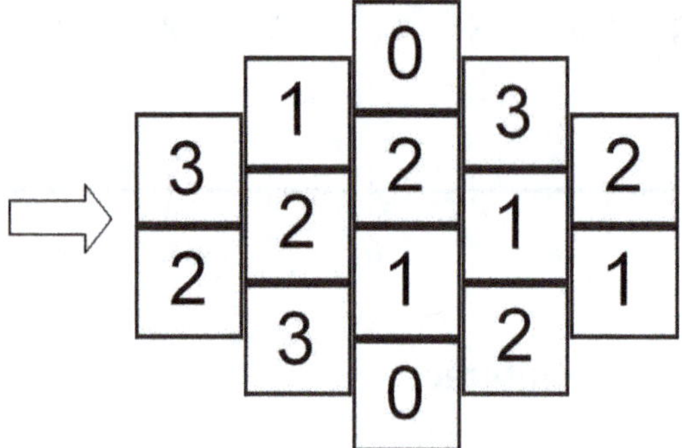

2. Subtract from 9.

9 – ________ = 8

9 – ________ = 2

9 – ________ = 4

9 – ________ = 6

9 – ________ = 5

9 – ________ = 3

9 – ________ = 0

9 – ________ = 1

9 – ________ = 9

3.

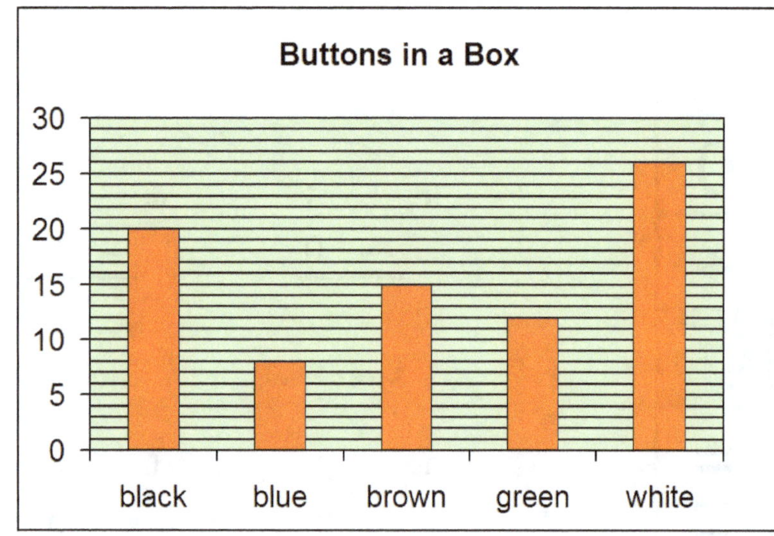

a. How many black and blue buttons are there in total? ________

b. How many fewer blue buttons are in the box than green buttons? ________

4. Mary is putting 8 pieces of fruit in a bowl. Some are apples and some are bananas. How many apples and how many bananas *could* she put in the bowl? Fill in the chart.

(apple)	1						
(banana)	7						
Total	8	8	8	8	8	8	8

Skills Review 35

1. Some children were collecting shells at the beach.

	Tally Marks
Brad	𝍸 𝍸 II
Carrie	𝍸 II
Eva	𝍸 III
Nelson	𝍸 𝍸 I

a. How many fewer shells did Carrie collect than Nelson? _________

b. How many did Carrie and Eva collect together? _______________

c. How many did Brad and Nelson collect together? _______________

2. Write <, > or =.

a. 8 + 2 ☐ 10 – 0 **b.** 6 + 3 ☐ 5 + 5 **c.** 7 – 3 ☐ 5 – 2

d. 9 – 7 ☐ 5 – 4 **e.** 6 – 3 ☐ 9 – 6 **f.** 5 + 4 ☐ 3 + 7

3. Find ways through the maze so that the sum of the numbers is 10.
Hint: Start with the 1 or 2 next to the arrow.

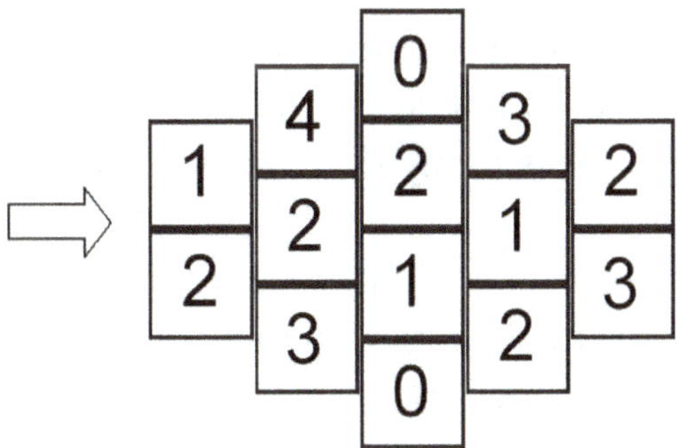

4. Solve the problems.

a. Mom had 10 roses on her rose bush. She picked 6 of them. How many roses were left on the bush?
b. Adam found 4 socks under the bed, 5 socks in the doghouse, and 1 in a shoe. How many socks did Adam find?

Skills Review 36

1. Using the color guide, color the fish that has the answer to the subtraction problem. You may color the rest of the picture, too.

7 – 2 – 4 = green
9 – 3 – 1 = blue
10 – 2 – 2 = red
8 – 1 – 4 = yellow
5 – 0 – 1 = brown

2. Draw a line to the correct answer.

	3 + 3	
	10 – 4	
	9 – 2	
	5 + 1	
6	9 – 3	**7**
	3 + 4	
	8 – 1	
	2 + 5	
	6 – 0	

3. Solve the problems.

a. Andy has 40 crayons. Denise has 50 crayons. How many do they have together?
b. Laura was supposed to wash 40 spoons. She washed 30 — but then here comes Mama with 20 more! How many does she still have to wash?
c. There were 9 puppies in a box. Then, two puppies jumped out of the box. Later, 3 more puppies jumped out. How many puppies stayed in the box?

4. Circle true or false.

a. 10 – 6 – 2 = 3	True	False	**b.** 5 + 5 + 0 = 10	True	False
c. 3 + 3 + 3 = 9	True	False	**d.** 9 – 4 – 1 = 4	True	False
e. 8 – 3 – 4 = 2	True	False	**f.** 2 + 5 + 1 = 8	True	False

Skills Review 37

1. Solve. Compare the two problems and their results.

a.	b.	c.
6 − 2 − 1 = _____	10 − 5 − 3 = _____	8 − 4 − 3 = _____
6 − 2 − 2 = _____	10 − 4 − 3 = _____	7 − 4 − 3 = _____

2. Circle two numbers with a red crayon if they make 9. Circle two numbers with a blue crayon if they make 10. Note: Each number can only be circled once.

5	4	5	5	6	4
3	7	0	6	3	5
5	6	9	1	8	5
5	3	4	4	9	1
2	8	9	0	7	3

3. Draw the hour hand on each clock. Write the time that the clock will show an hour later.

	a. half past two	b. nine o'clock	c. five o'clock	d. half past six
An hour later →	__________	__________	__________	__________

4. Annie is baking a cake. The cake needs to bake for half an hour. If she puts it in the oven at 3 o'clock, at what time will it be done?

Skills Review 38

1. Practice adding and subtracting.

a. 53 + 10 = _______	**b.** 97 – 30 = _______
c. 20 + 70 = _______	**d.** 100 – 80 = _______
e. 49 – 20 = _______	**f.** 10 + 60 = _______

2. Write the time in two ways: (1) using the expressions *o'clock* or *half past* and (2) with numbers.

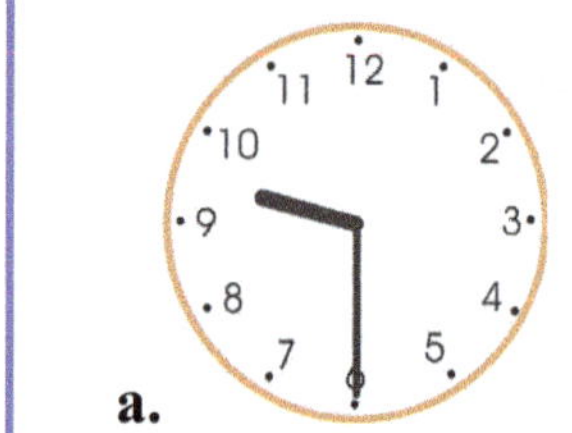 **a.**	 **b.**	 **c.**	 **d.**
half past ______	______ o'clock	half past ______	______ o'clock
_____ : ________	_____ : _______	_____ : _______	_____ : _______

3. How many hours pass?

a. From 3:00 to 7:00 ______ hour(s) **b.** From 10:00 to 12:00 ______ hour(s)

c. From 5:30 to 6:00 ______ hours(s) **d.** From 2:00 to 8:00 ______ hour(s)

4. Subtract many numbers.

a. 7 – 1 – 3 – 2 = ________	**b.** 10 – 4 – 2 – 1 = ________

5. Amanda has 20 dolls and Cassy has 10 dolls. How many fewer dolls does Cassy have than Amanda?

6. Justin and Deanna spent an hour catching fireflies in the yard. If they started at 7:30, what time did they finish?

Skills Review 39

1. Add or subtract in your head. Then color using the color guide.

5 = yellow
6 = purple
7 = red
8 = orange
9 = pink
10 = blue

2. Write the time a half-hour later and another half-hour later. Use numbers.

Now it is:	**a.** 8:00	**b.** 3:30	**c.** 11:00	**d.** 5:30	**e.** 1:30
1/2 hour later it is:					
another 1/2 hour later:					

3. Circle the event that takes a longer time.

a. Play a board game.	Make your bed.	**b.** Draw a flower.	Wash your hair.
c. Color a picture.	Drink a glass of water.	**d.** Eat a cookie.	Eat a raisin.

4. Fifty ants were carrying a cracker across the ground. Ten ants decided the cracker was too heavy and left. How many ants were still carrying the cracker?

5. Nine turtles were lying in the sun. Two of them decided to go swimming. Then three more decided to go swimming. How many turtles were still lying in the sun?

Skills Review 40

1. Write the time an hour later. Use numbers.

Now it is:	**a.** 4:00	**b.** 9:30	**c.** 6:30	**d.** 1:00	**e.** 3:30
An hour later it is:					

2. Write $<$, $>$ or $=$.

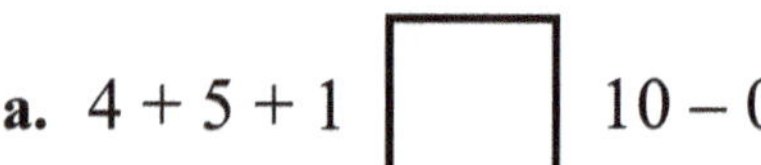

a. $4 + 5 + 1$ ☐ $10 - 0$ **b.** $1 + 0 + 2$ ☐ $5 - 3 - 2$ **c.** $6 - 4$ ☐ $3 + 1$

d. $8 - 3 - 2$ ☐ $6 + 1$ **e.** $9 - 1 - 0$ ☐ $3 + 3 + 2$ **f.** $4 + 4$ ☐ $9 - 2$

3. Draw the hour and minute hands on the clock so it matches the situation. Then write the time, including AM or PM.

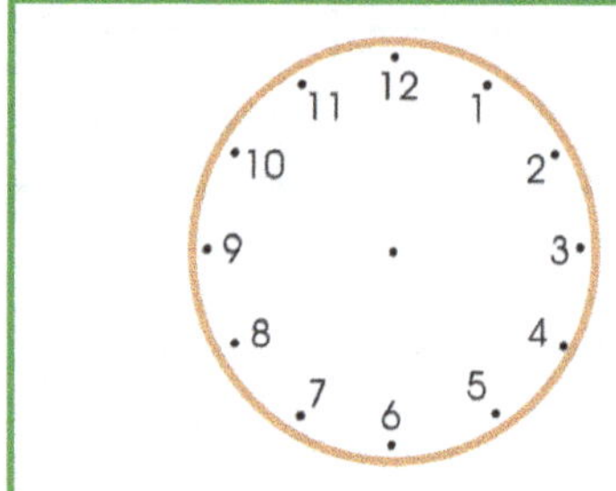

a. I do schoolwork.

____ : ____ ____

b. I eat breakfast.

____ : ____ ____

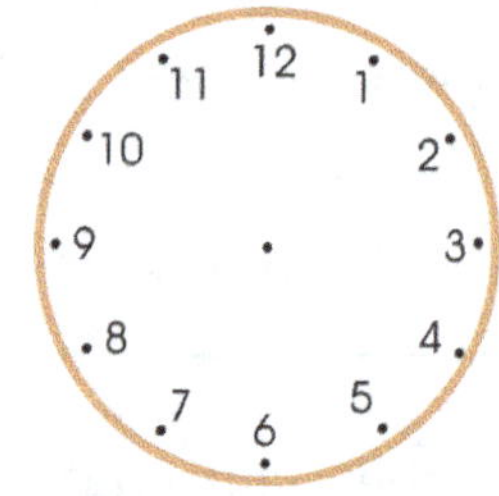

c. I go to bed.

____ : ____ ____

4. Add the words *yesterday*, *today*, and *tomorrow*. The events are not in order.

__________________, Peter will go to the dentist.

__________________, Peter had a toothache.

__________________, Peter's mom calls to make an appointment.

5. Susan collected 40 pretty leaves, and Lindsay collected 60 leaves and 10 acorns. How many *leaves* did the two girls collect in total?

Skills Review 41

1. Add or subtract.

a.	b.	c.	d.	e.	f.
$1 + 9$	$6 - 3$	$0 + 4$	$10 - 7$	$5 + 2$	$8 - 6$

2. Tanya goes to the beach on Saturdays. What dates will she go to the beach in August?

August ________ August ________

August ________ August ________

August ________

August

Su	Mo	Tu	We	Th	Fr	Sa
						1
2	3	4	5	6	7	8
9	10	11	12	13	14	15
16	17	18	19	20	21	22
23	24	25	26	27	28	29
30	31					

3. Circle the event that takes a longer time.

a. Turn on the light. Open the door.	**b.** Bake a cake. Fry an egg.
c. Put on a shirt. Tie your shoes.	**d.** Watch a movie. Eat lunch.

4. Write the names of the two months that follow the given month.

a. January ________________ ________________

b. July ________________ ________________

c. October ________________ ________________

5. Rachel baked 5 apple pies, 2 pumpkin pies, and 2 cherry pies.

a. How many pies did Rachel bake in total?

b. Rachel's cat jumped on the table and chased a mouse through 3 of the pies! How many good pies does Rachel have left?

Skills Review 42

1. Carla picked some vegetables in her garden. Draw the bars for the bar graph.

tomatoes	17
peppers	9
cucumbers	12
eggplants	7

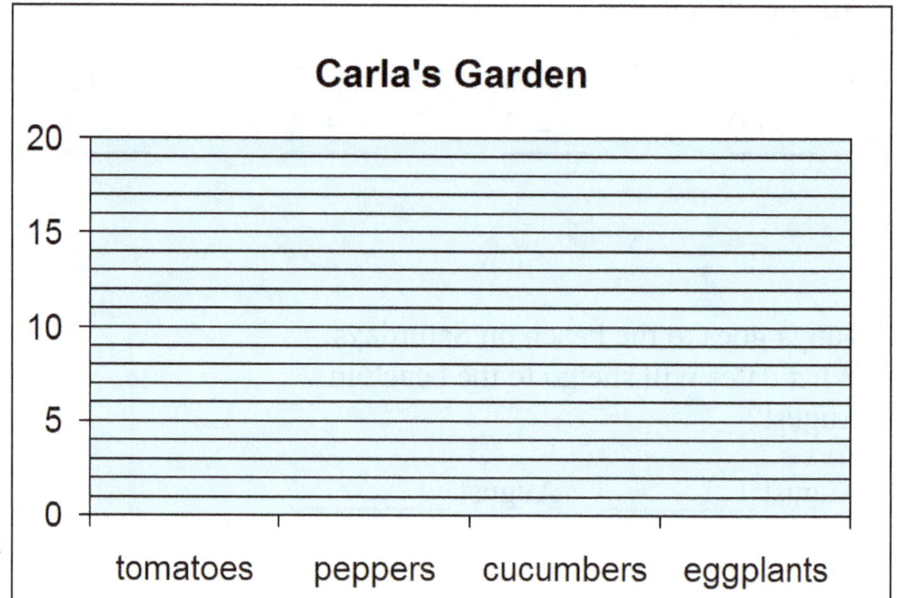

a. How many peppers and eggplant did Carla pick in total?

____

b. How many more cucumbers did Carla pick than eggplant? ____________

2. Wow! Twenty butterflies just landed on Tom's hat! Then, ten butterflies flew away. How many butterflies are still on Tom's hat?

3. Write down how many corners each shape has.

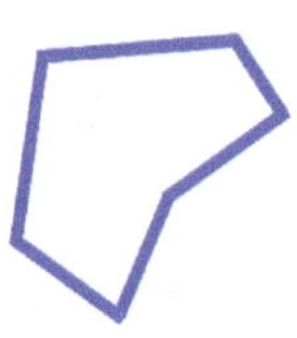

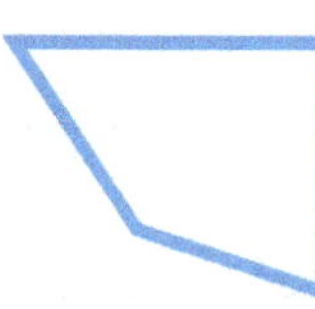

a. _____ **b.** _____ **c.** _____ **d.** _____ **e.** _____

4. AM or PM? Draw a line from each situation to the correct answer.

Daddy eats lunch.	AM	Look at the fireflies!
It is bedtime.		What is for breakfast?
I get up.	PM	What a pretty sunset!

Skills Review 43

1. Find all of the MONDAYS in May on the calendar. Write their dates below:

May _____ May _____

May _____ May _____

May

Su	Mo	Tu	We	Th	Fr	Sa
					1	2
3	4	5	6	7	8	9
10	11	12	13	14	15	16
17	18	19	20	21	22	23
24	25	26	27	28	29	30
31						

2. Circle the event that takes a longer time.

a. Climb a hill. Climb a mountain.	**b.** Take a bath. Make a sandwich.

3. Using a ruler, draw a line from dot to dot so that you divide the shape into <u>two new shapes</u>. How many sides do the new shapes have? How many corners?

a. The new shapes have _______ sides,

and _______ corners.

They are ________________________

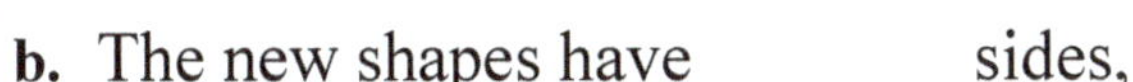

b. The new shapes have _______ sides,

and _______ corners.

They are ________________________

4. Answer the questions. Hint: Make the shapes yourself using your shape cut-outs from the printable cut-outs at the end of this worktext.

a. Adam is playing with his shape cut-outs. He wants to make a pentagon. What is one way he could make one?
He could put together a

____

and a ___________________________ .

b. Adam decided to make a hexagon. He put together a pink rectangle and a red triangle.

1. Did he make a hexagon?

2. If no, what kind of shape did he make?

Skills Review 44

1. Color the shapes using the color guide.

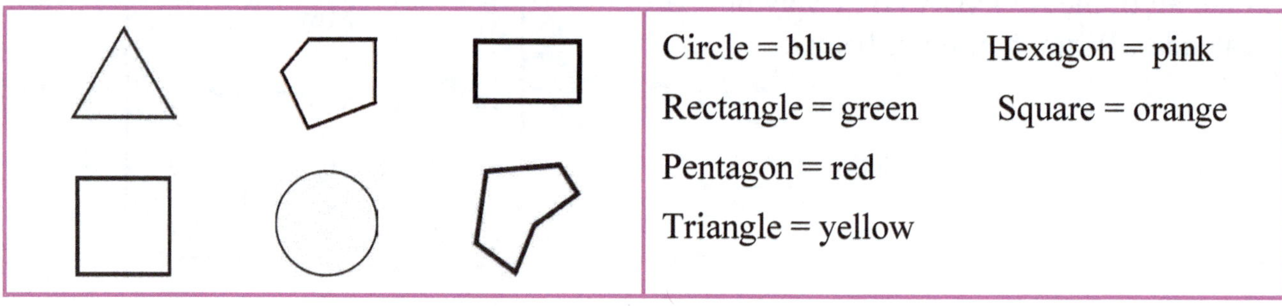

Circle = blue
Hexagon = pink
Rectangle = green
Square = orange
Pentagon = red
Triangle = yellow

2. Tell when the event happens.

   a. You can see the stars in the sky. ______________________________

   b. The school day begins. ______________________________

   c. Mom washes the lunch dishes. ______________________________

3. Draw three dots anywhere in this space. Join the dots with lines. Use a ruler! What shape did you get?

4. Write the time in two ways: (1) using the expressions *o'clock* or *half past* and (2) with numbers.

a. ______ o'clock _____ : _______	**b.** half past ______ _____ : _______
c. ______ o'clock _____ : _______	**d.** half past ______ _____ : _______

Skills Review 45

1. Continue the skip-counting patterns.

a. 83, 85, 87, ________, ________, ________, ________, ________

b. 23, 27, 31 , ________, ________, ________, ________, ________

2. Repeat the pattern to fill the grid.

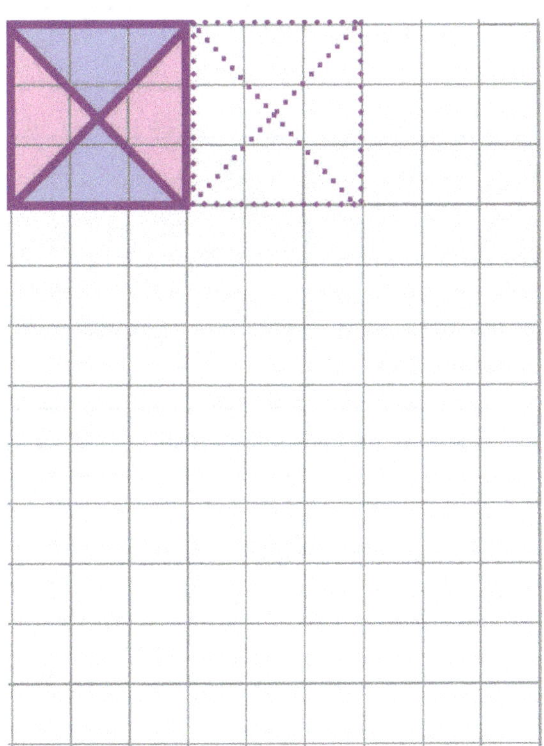

3. Put the events in order.
Mark 1, 2, and 3.

Mama and babies go for a walk.
The eggs hatch.
Mama Hen is sitting on her eggs.

4. Adam kept a tally of how many times he made different kinds of shapes with his shape cut-outs.

a. How many pentagons and rectangles did he make in total? __________

b. Which shape do you think was his favorite shape to make? ____________________

c. How many more quadrilaterals did he make than rectangles? __________

	Tally Marks
Pentagon	𝍸 𝍸 𝍸 𝍸
Hexagon	𝍸 𝍸 III
Rectangle	𝍸 III
Quadrilateral	𝍸 𝍸 II

Skills Review 46

1. Look at the calendar and answer the questions.

October

Su	Mo	Tu	We	Th	Fr	Sa
				1	2	3
4	5	6	7	8	9	10
11	12	13	14	15	16	17
18	19	20	21	22	23	24
25	26	27	28	29	30	31

a. What day of the week is October 20?

____

b. What date is the first Monday after October 22?

____

2. Write below each shape what part of it is shaded.

a. 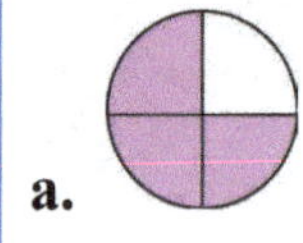	**b.** 	**c.** 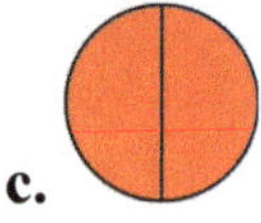	**d.** 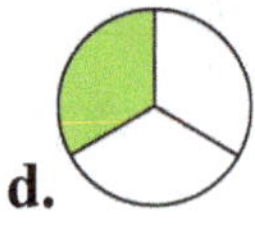
__________	__________	__________	__________
__________	__________	__________	__________

3. Write $<$, $>$ or $=$.

a. $50 + 40$ ☐ $100 - 10$ **b.** $60 - 20$ ☐ $20 + 10$  **c.** $80 - 30$ ☐ $60 + 10$

4. Circle AM or PM.

a. I watch the sunset.	**b.** Breakfast smells yummy!	**c.** Daddy's home from work!
AM PM	AM PM	AM PM

5. Some children were selling tickets to a school play.

a. How many tickets did David and Madison sell altogether? _______

b. How many fewer tickets did Ryan sell than Kendra? _______

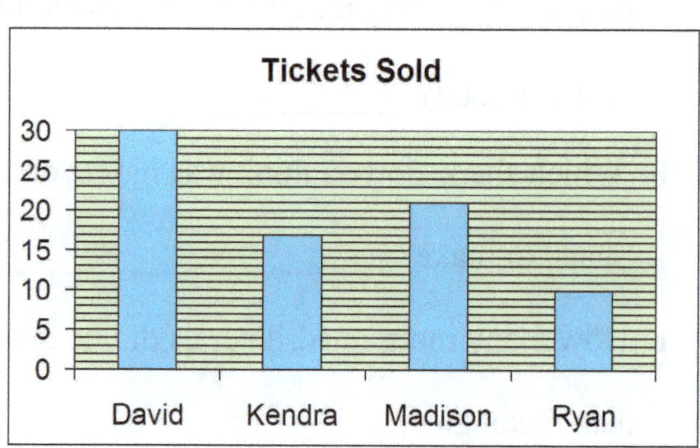

Skills Review 47

1. Write < , > or = .

a. 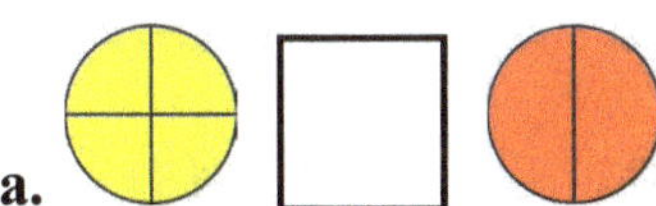

b. 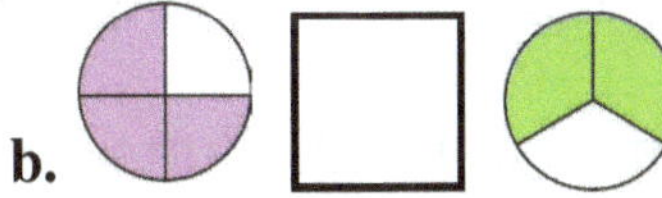

c. 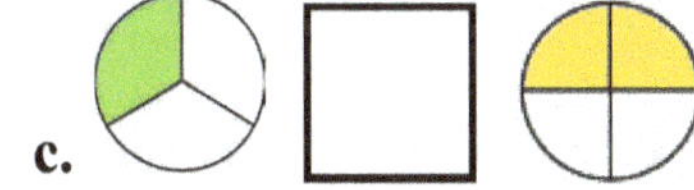

2. Continue the pattern on the grid.

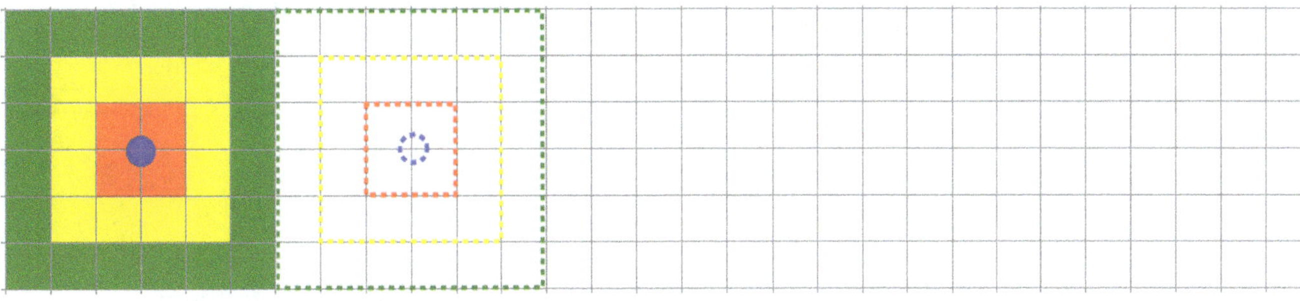

3. Carlos has 60 baseball cards. Ricky has 40 baseball cards. How many baseball cards do the two boys have in total?

4. The Hill family arrived at the beach at 8:30 am. They left two hours later. What time did they leave?

5. Compare the toys to the "measuring stick." Mark the <u>longer</u> of the two.

Skills Review 48

1. How many hours pass?

   a. From 2:00 to 7:00 ______ hour(s) **b.** From 8:00 to 12:00 ______ hour(s)

   c. From 9:00 to 11:30 ______ hours(s) **d.** From 3:00 to 9:00 ______ hour(s)

2. Add or subtract.

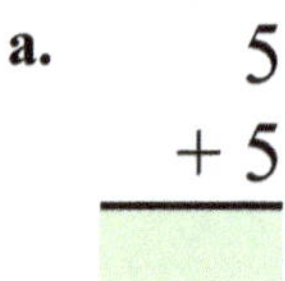

a.	**b.**	**c.**	**d.**	**e.**	**f.**
5	7	9	8	6	4
+ 5	− 4	+ 0	− 3	+ 2	− 0

3. Order these things from lightest to heaviest by writing 1, 2, and 3 next to them.

4. Divide these shapes by drawing straight lines from dot to dot. Then color them as the instructions say.

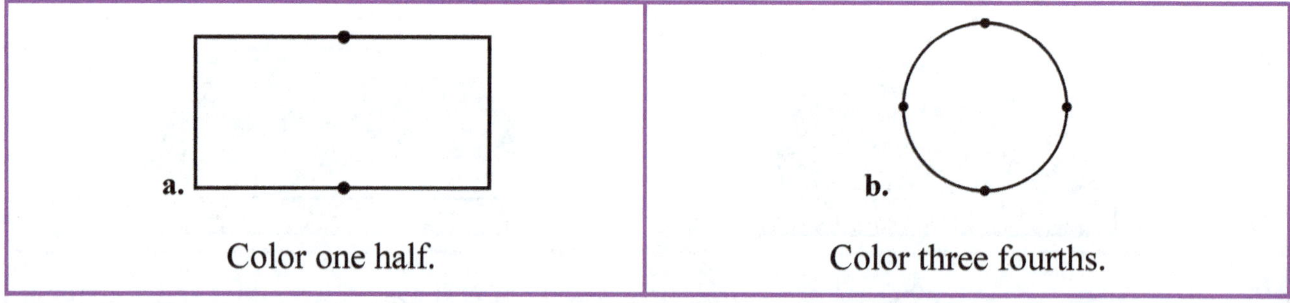

5. Twenty monkeys were swinging on vines. Then, ten of the monkeys left to find some bananas. Later, four more monkeys left. How many monkeys were still swinging on vines?

Skills Review 49

1. Four kittens were lying in the sun, three kittens were climbing a tree, and two kittens were hiding in Daddy's boot. How many kittens were there in total?

2. Write the time using numbers.

a. ______ : ______	**b.** ______ : ______	**c.** ______ : ______	**d.** ______ : ______

3. How many paperclips long are these insects?

a.

b.

c.

4. Fill in the missing numbers.

a. 90 – ________ = 60	**b.** ________ – 20 = 50	**c.** 80 + 20 = ________
d. ________ + 40 = 80	**e.** 30 + ________ = 70	**f.** 100 – 10 = ________

Skills Review 50

1. How many inches long are these items?

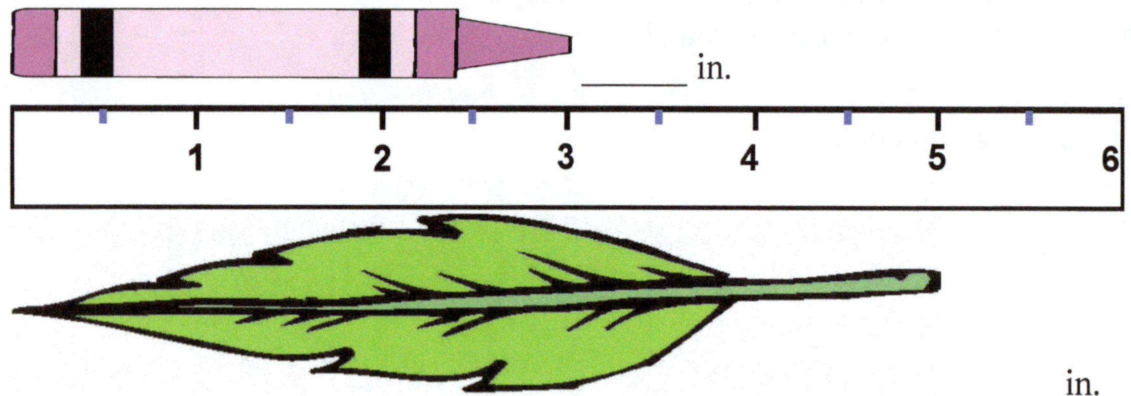

______ in.

______ in.

2. Continue the skip-counting pattern.

53, 55, 57, ________, ________, ________, ________, ________

3. Solve. Compare the two problems and their results.

a.	b.	c.
9 − 4 − 1 = _____	10 − 2 − 3 = _____	7 − 3 − 2 = _____
9 − 4 − 2 = _____	10 − 3 − 3 = _____	6 − 3 − 2 = _____

4. Using a ruler, draw a line from dot to dot so that you divide the shape into two new shapes. How many sides do the new shapes have? How many corners?

a. The new shapes have _______ sides,

and _______ corners.

They are ______________________

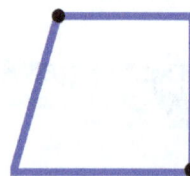

b. The new shapes have _______ sides,

and _______ corners.

They are ______________________

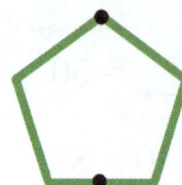

Skills Review 51

1. Use a ruler and draw lines with these lengths:

a. 6 in.

b. 12 cm

2. Complete. Then draw lines to connect the facts from the same fact family.

_____ − 8 = 2	7 − 4 = _____	9 − 5 = _____
3 + _____ = 7	_____ + 1 = 6	4 + _____ = 7
9 − _____ = 5	10 − 2 = _____	2 + 8 = _____
_____ + 2 = 9	4 + _____ = 9	9 − 7 = _____
6 − 5 = _____	9 − _____ = 7	5 + 1 = _____

3. Complete the drawings to make a...

a. ...pentagon.

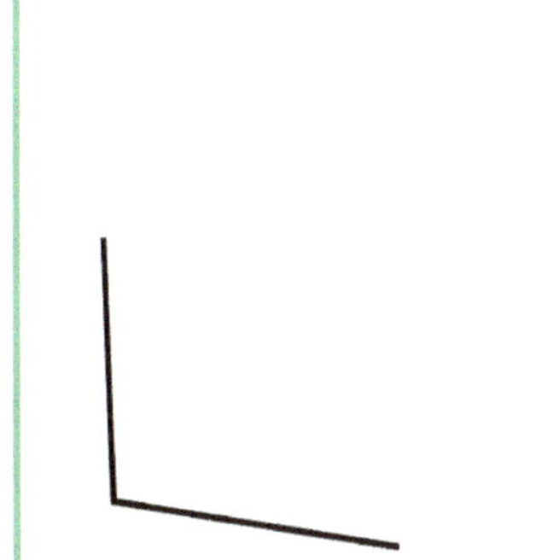

b. ...hexagon.

4. Circle the event that takes a longer time.

a. Give the dog a bath. Read a poem.	**b.** Bake a cake. Eat an ice cream cone.

Skills Review 52

1. How many centimeters long are these things?

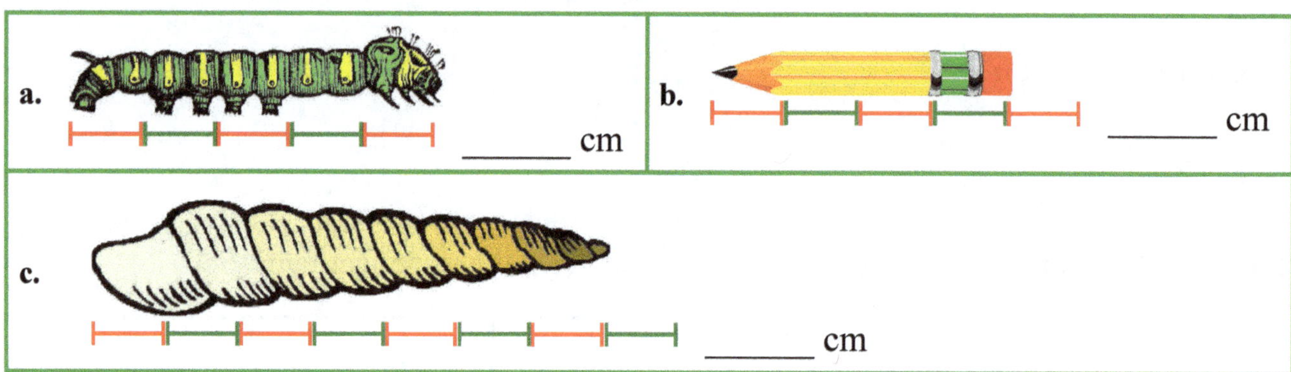

2. Fill in either "AM" or "PM."

a. The stars are shining. It's 1 _____.
b. Almost time to cook lunch. It's 10:30 _____.
c. Corey is eating breakfast. It's 8 _____.
d. It's really hot outside! It's 12 _____.

3. Match the objects with their shape.

box

cylinder

cube

ball

4. Vanessa needs 70 beads to make a necklace. Right now, she has 30 beads. How many more beads does she need?

5. Write the addition or subtraction that matches the number line jumps.

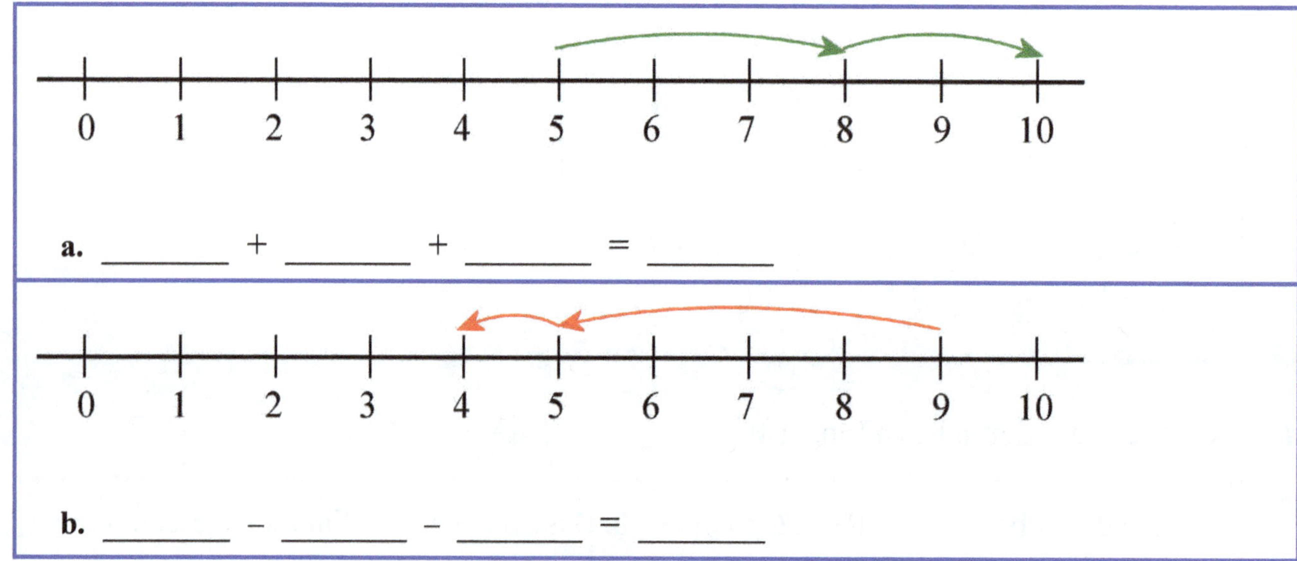

Skills Review 53

1. Measure the sides of the shapes and write their lengths.

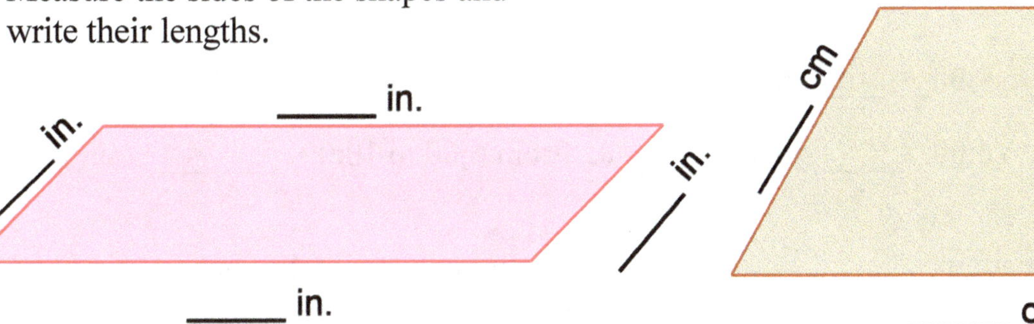

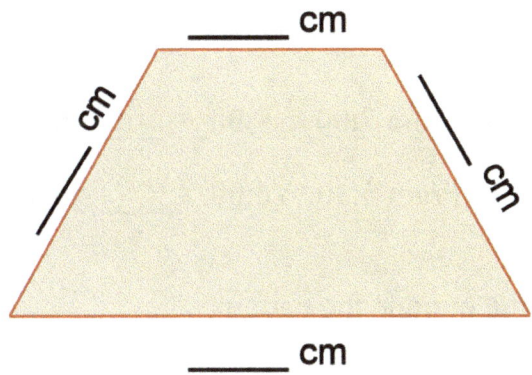

2. Add. Compare the problems.

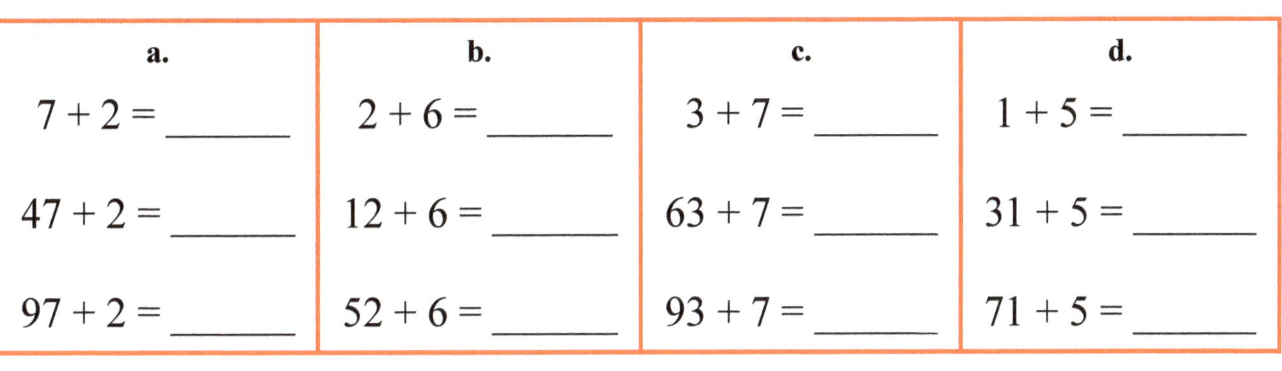

a.	b.	c.	d.
7 + 2 = _____	2 + 6 = _____	3 + 7 = _____	1 + 5 = _____
47 + 2 = _____	12 + 6 = _____	63 + 7 = _____	31 + 5 = _____
97 + 2 = _____	52 + 6 = _____	93 + 7 = _____	71 + 5 = _____

3. Write < , > or = .

a. 8 + 0 + 1 ☐ 10 – 1 – 1   b. 9 – 2 – 4 ☐ 2 + 1 + 3

c. 6 + 3 + 1 ☐ 4 + 3 + 3   d. 0 + 7 + 1 ☐ 9 – 0 – 2

4. Divide these shapes by drawing straight lines from dot to dot. Then color them as the given amount. Color …

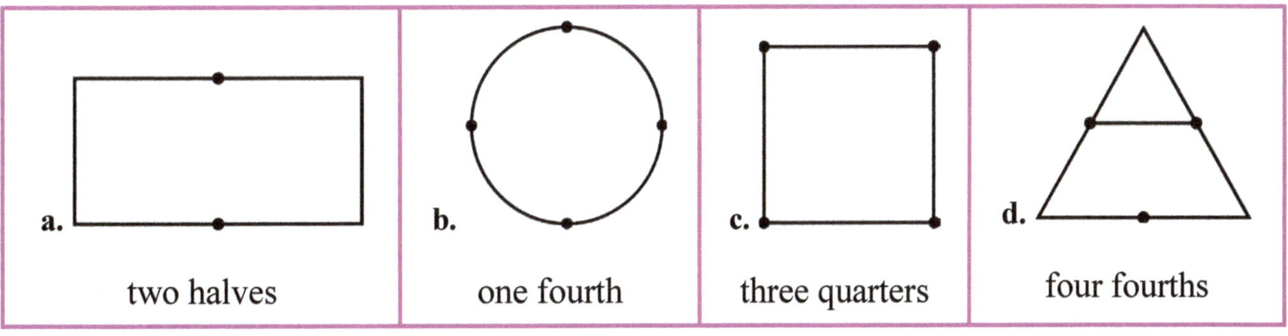

Skills Review 54

1. How many hours pass?

a. From 7:00 to 9:00 ______ hour(s)

b. From 11:00 to 12:00 ______ hour(s)

c. From 5:30 to 6:00 ______ hours(s)

d. From 6:00 to 10:00 ______ hour(s)

2. Continue the pattern.

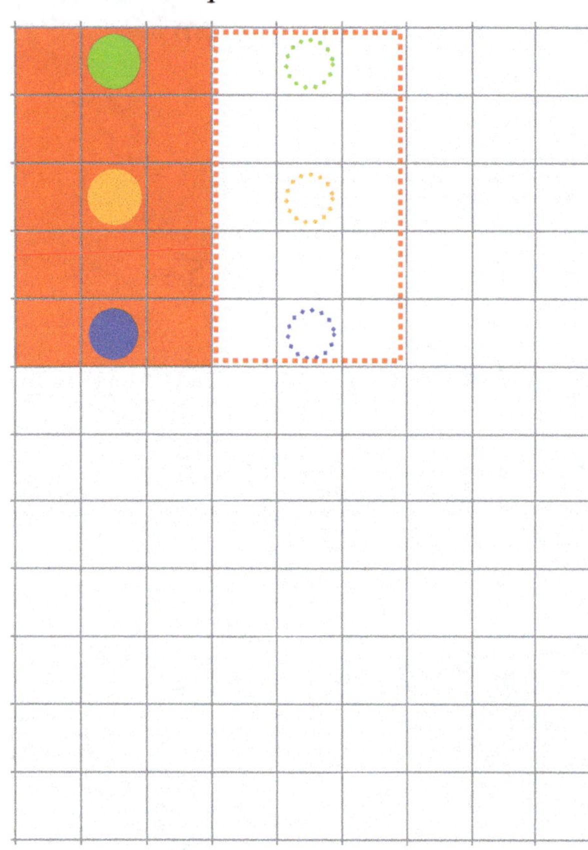

3. Are these things in the shape of a *box* or a *cube*? Underline the right choice.

a.

box *or* cube

b.

box *or* cube

4. Are these things in the shape of a *cylinder* or a *ball*? Underline the right choice.

a.

cylinder *or* ball

b.

cylinder *or* ball

5. Write the numbers in the boxes. Add the ones in their own column.

a. 14 + 2

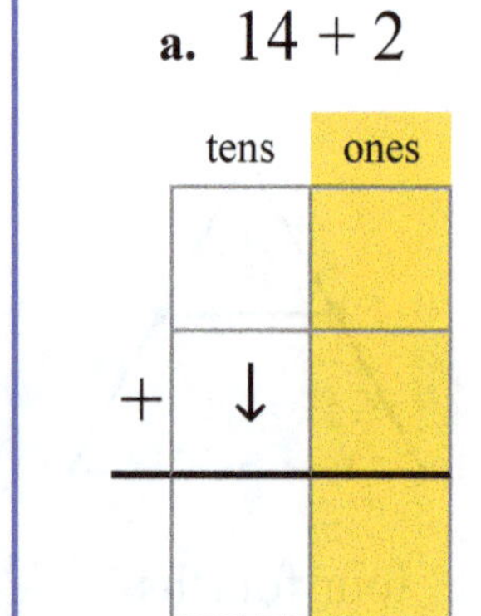

b. 53 + 5

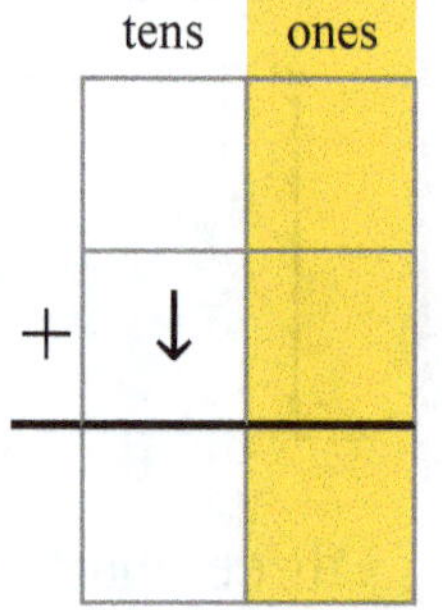

c. 81 + 3

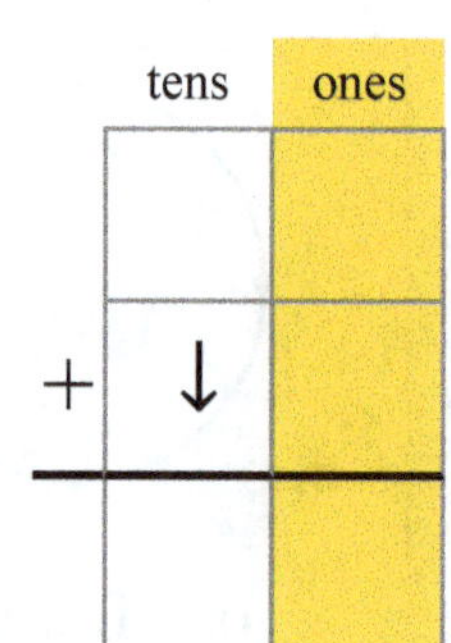

d. 72 + 6

tens ones

\+ ↓

Skills Review 55

1. Continue the pattern.

95 – 2 = _____

85 – 2 = _____

75 – 2 = _____

____ – _____ = _____

____ – _____ = _____

____ – _____ = _____

____ – _____ = _____

____ – _____ = _____

2. Write down how many corners each shape has.

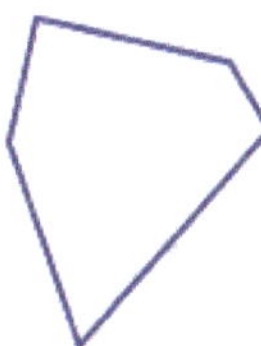

a. _____

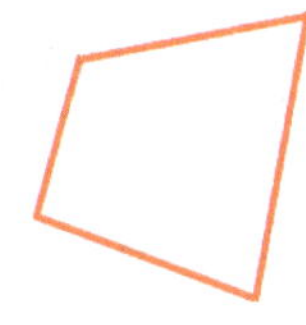

b. _____

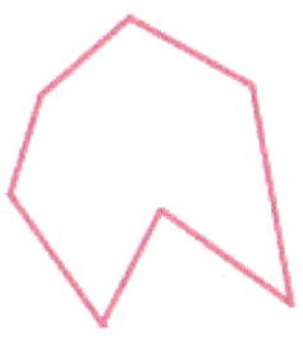

c. _____

3. Sharon saw 35 butterflies and 15 ladybugs in her garden. How many more butterflies than ladybugs did she see?

4. Mike has to practice playing his trumpet for half an hour. If he starts practicing at 10:30, what time will he finish?

5. Add the words *yesterday*, *today*, and *tomorrow*. The events are not in order.

____________________, Bill is painting his house.

____________________, Bill's house will look very different!

____________________, Bill bought some paint.

6. Add three numbers.

a.	b.	c.
71 + 3 + 5 = _____	94 + 2 + 1 = _____	100 + 4 + 2 = _____
43 + 2 + 3 = _____	81 + 6 + 3 = _____	63 + 1 + 3 = _____

Skills Review 56

1. Carol and Brian were making mud pies in the yard.
   Carol made 15 mud pies and Brian made 5.
   How many fewer mud pies did Brian make?

2. Measure the sides of the shape and mark their lengths.

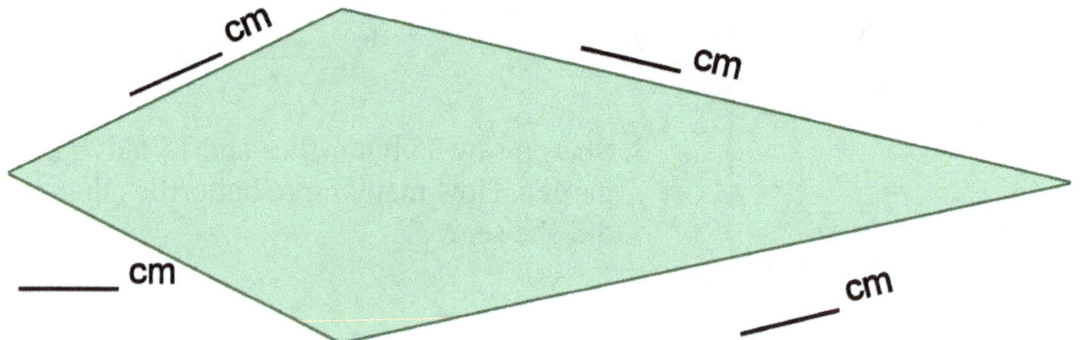

3. Write the numbers in the boxes. Subtract the tens and the ones in their columns.

a. 63 – 42 **b.** 82 – 31 **c.** 77 – 4 **d.** 42 – 11

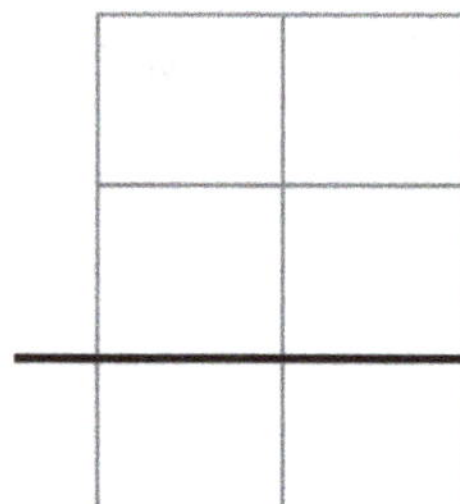
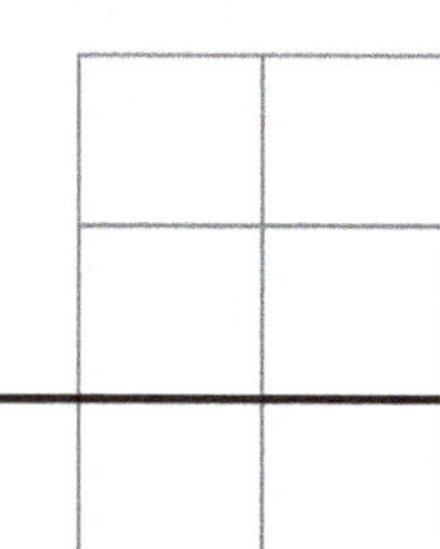
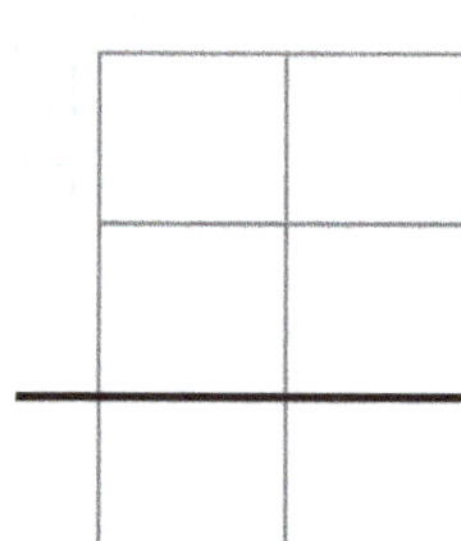
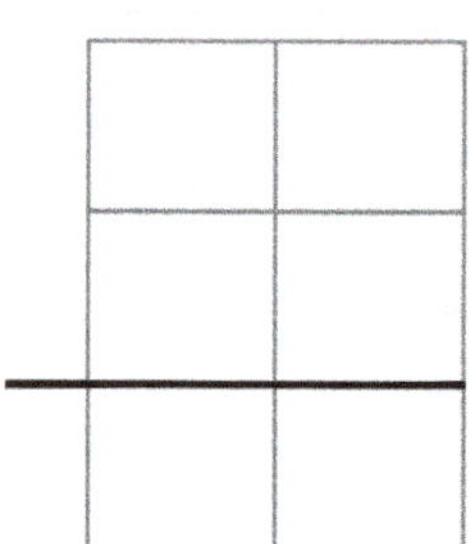

4. Do the tally marks match the bar graph? If not, correct the tally.

	Tally Marks
Hamsters	𝍸 ||
Goldfish	𝍸 𝍸 𝍸 𝍸 |||
Kittens	𝍸 |||
Puppies	𝍸 𝍸 ||
Parakeets	𝍸 𝍸

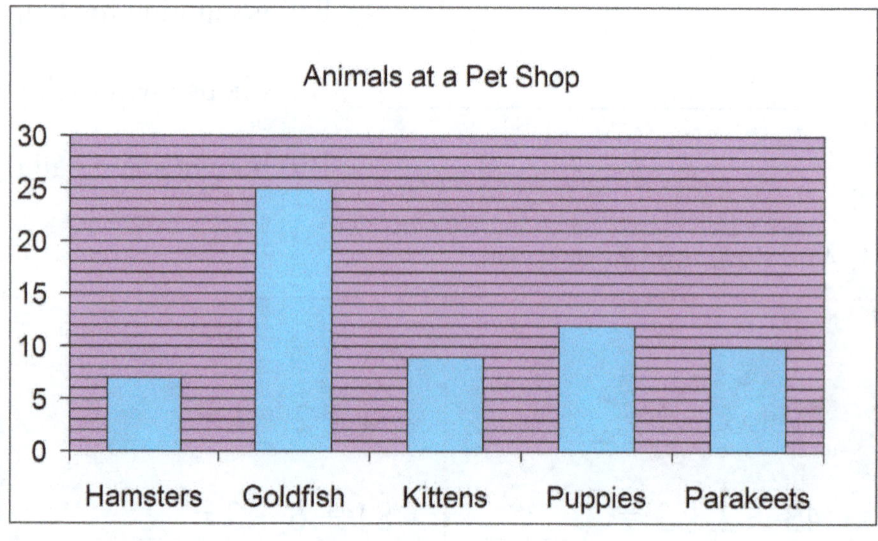

Skills Review 57

1. Find all the TUESDAYS in July.
   Write their dates below.

   July _______ July _______

   July _______ July _______

July

Su	Mo	Tu	We	Th	Fr	Sa
			1	2	3	4
5	6	7	8	9	10	11
12	13	14	15	16	17	18
19	20	21	22	23	24	25
26	27	28	29	30	31	

2. True or false? If the addition or subtraction is true, color the box light blue.
   If it is false, color the box yellow.

a. $41 + 30 = 74$	**b.** $59 - 40 = 21$	**c.** $22 + 70 = 92$
d. $82 - 30 = 52$	**e.** $20 + 15 = 35$	**f.** $74 - 20 = 54$
g. $102 - 60 = 32$	**h.** $63 + 20 = 83$	**i.** $91 - 50 = 41$

3. Order these things from lightest to heaviest by writing 1, 2, and 3 next to them.

a.

b.

4. Complete the next ten.

a. $31 + \bigcirc = 40$	**b.** $95 + \bigcirc = 100$	**c.** $43 + \bigcirc = 50$
d. $67 + \bigcirc = 70$	**e.** $82 + \bigcirc = 90$	**f.** $26 + \bigcirc = 30$

Skills Review 58

1. Mary’s garden has lots of flowers.

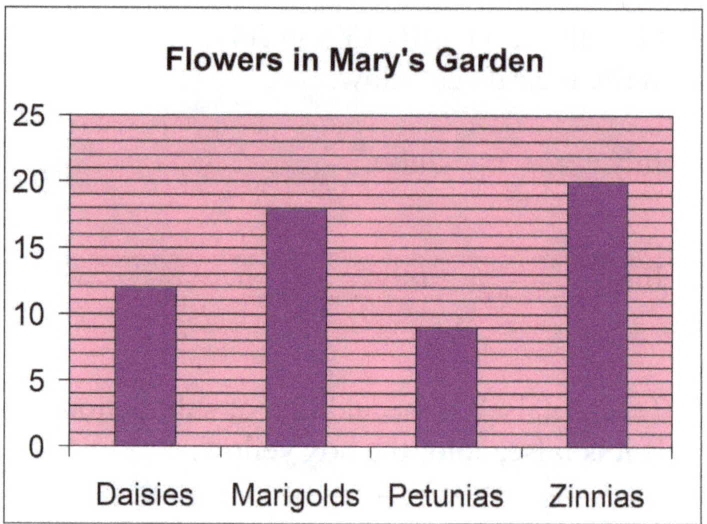

   a. How many zinnias and daisies does she have, in total? _______

   b. How many more daisies does she have than petunias? _______

   c. Make up one more question about the graph and tell it to your teacher.

2. Complete. Split the second number into two parts so that you can complete the next ten.

a. 59 + 4	**b.** 98 + 5	**c.** 47 + 6
59 + ____ + ____	98 + ____ + ____	47 + ____ + ____
60 + ____ = ______	______ + ____ = ______	______ + ____ = ______

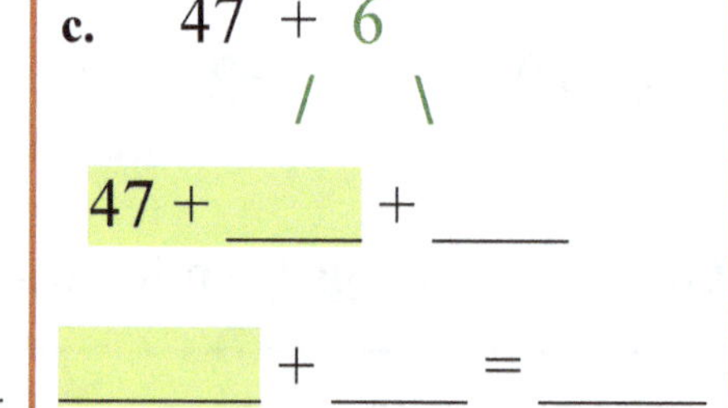

3. Oh no! Thirty blackbirds are eating Mama’s pumpkin pies! Ten of them flew away, but then fifteen more blackbirds arrived. How many blackbirds are eating pumpkin pie now?

4. Damon played basketball for two hours. If it was 6 o’clock when he stopped playing, what time did he start?

5. Subtract.

a.	**b.**	**c.**	**d.**
45 – 2 = _____	94 – 3 = _____	16 – 4 = _____	29 – 3 = _____
19 – 6 = _____	67 – 5 = _____	78 – 7 = _____	33 – 2 = _____

Skills Review 59

1. Measure the sides of the shape and mark their lengths.

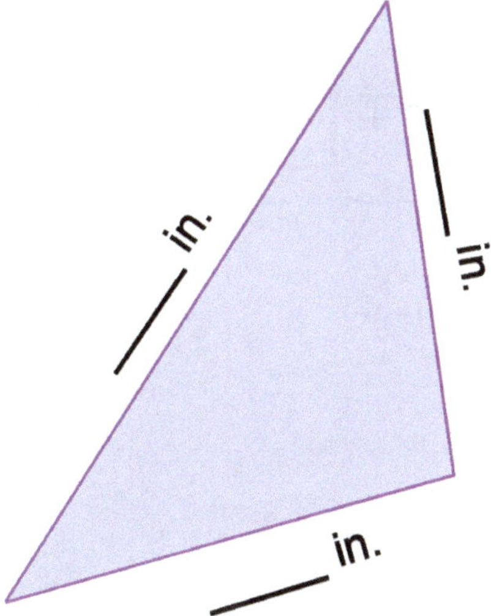

2. What three-dimensional shape do these objects have? Write it on the line.

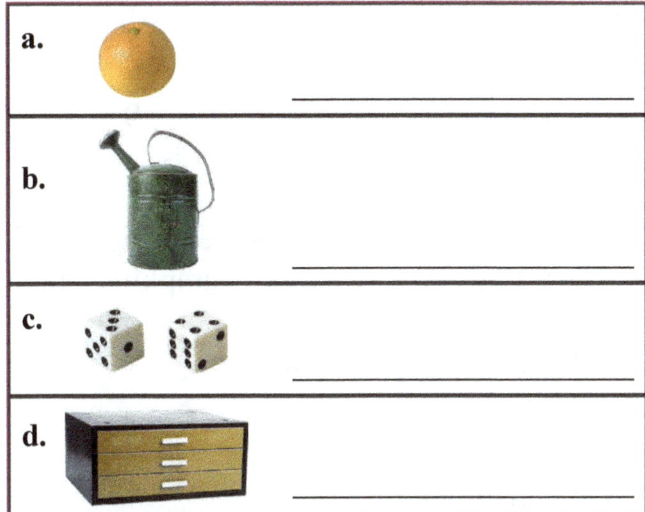

3. Subtract from whole tens.

a.	b.	c.	d.
60 – 4 = ______	90 – 9 = ______	50 – 4 = ______	70 – 6 = ______
60 – 3 = ______	90 – 5 = ______	50 – 5 = ______	70 – 8 = ______

4. Laura picked 50 strawberries. Then, she ate 20 of them. Later, a cow took 10 of her strawberries! How many strawberries did she have left?

5. Continue the skip-counting pattern.

97, 102, 107, ________, ________, ________, ________, ________

6. Compare. Write <, >, or = .

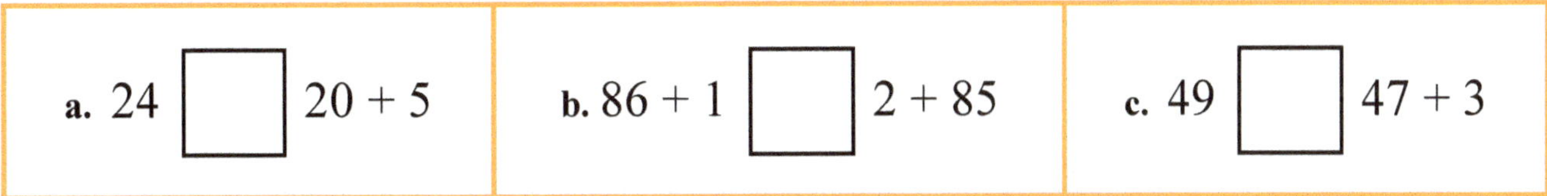

a. 24 ☐ 20 + 5	b. 86 + 1 ☐ 2 + 85	c. 49 ☐ 47 + 3

Skills Review 60

1. Find the missing numbers.

a.	**b.**	**c.**
5 + ☐ = 10	9 + ☐ = 10	7 + ☐ = 10
5 + ☐ = 11	9 + ☐ = 11	7 + ☐ = 11

2. Peggy Pig ate 9 pumpkins. Peter Pig ate 10 pumpkins.
   Then, Peggy ate two more pumpkins, and now she was really full!

   Who ate more pumpkins?

   How many more?

3. Add or subtract.

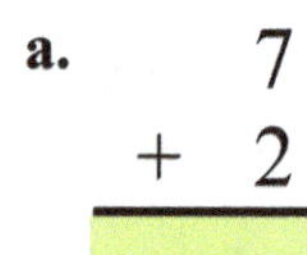

a. $7 + 2 =$ ☐ **b.** $10 - 6 =$ ☐ **c.** $8 - 0 =$ ☐ **d.** $4 + 3 =$ ☐ **e.** $5 + 5 =$ ☐

4. Adam is playing with his shape cut-outs again.
   This time, he wants to make an L-shape.

   a. What two shapes does he need to use?

   b. Draw the L-shape in this box.

Skills Review 61

1. Color the answers to the problems using the color guide. Then color the rest of the picture.

Green: 8 + 8, 6 + 7, 10 + 2

Blue: 7 + 8, 5 + 5

Red: 9 + 8

Yellow: 7 + 7

Pink: 9 + 2

2. Add. First make a new ten with some of the single dots.

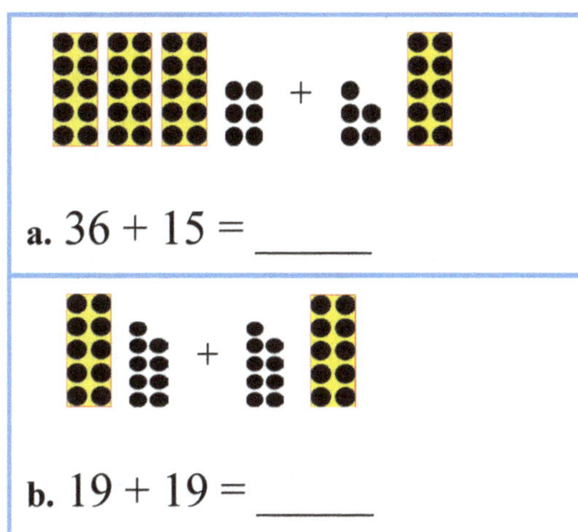

a. 36 + 15 = _____

b. 19 + 19 = _____

3. Add. Think how the nine or the eight wants to be ten! If the *second* number is 8 or 9, turn the addition around. You can add the numbers in the other order, 8 or 9 first.

a. 8 + 3 = ______ b. 8 + 9 = ______ c. 9 + 6 = ______

d. 5 + 8 = ______ e. 8 + 6 = ______ f. 9 + 5 = ______

4. Write either AM or PM for each situation.

a. Yummy! Mom is making spaghetti and meatballs! 	b. It's too early to get out of bed! 
c. In one more hour, it will be Susie's bedtime. 	d. Martin needs a flashlight because it's dark outside. 

Skills Review 62

1. Write the numbers in the boxes. Subtract the tens and the ones in their columns.

a. 65 – 33 **b.** 87 – 15 **c.** 48 – 5 **d.** 76 – 42

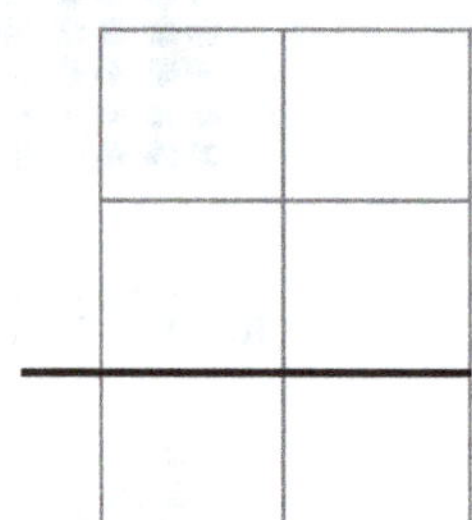
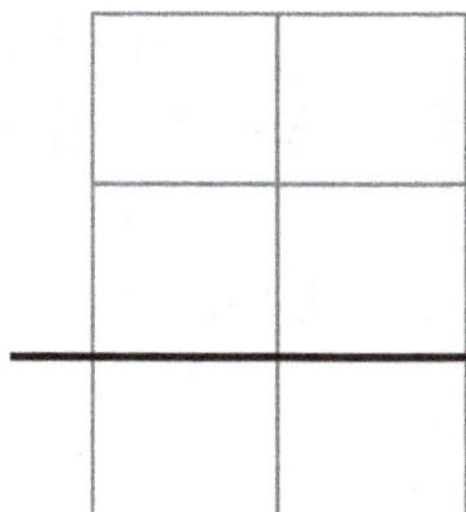

2. Fill in the missing numbers in the addition puzzle.

40	–		=	0
+				
	+	30	=	50
=		+		–
60				40
		=		=
90	–	80	=	

3. Measure the sides of the shape and write their lengths.

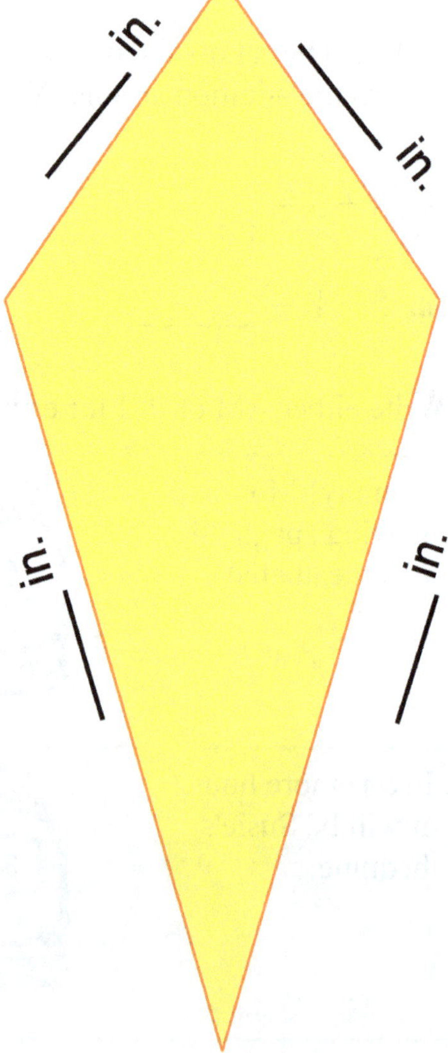

4. Alan planted 9 apple trees and 10 cherry trees. How many trees did Alan plant?

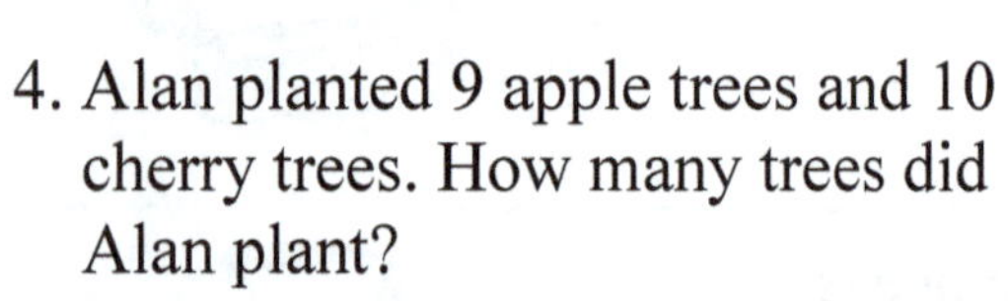

5. Twenty children took an English test. Thirteen of the children got a good score. How many children did not get a good score?

Skills Review 63

1. Write the time using numbers.

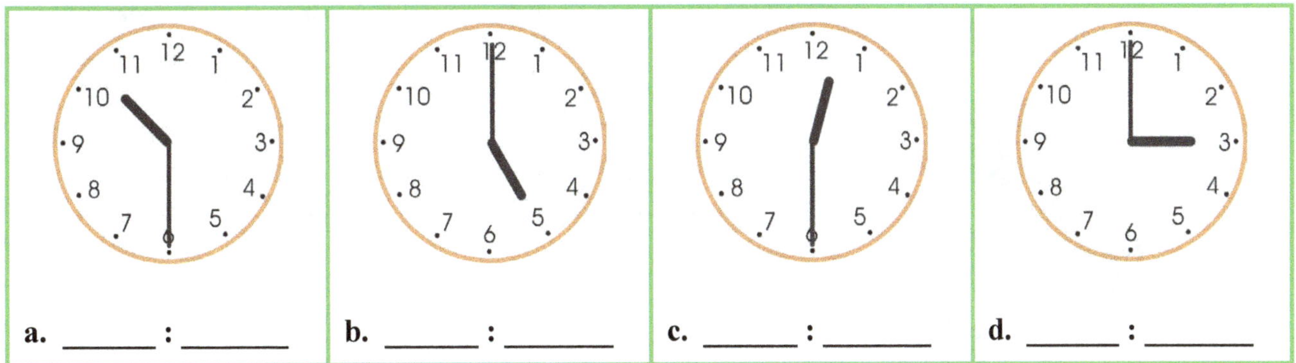

a. _____ : _____	b. _____ : _____	c. _____ : _____	d. _____ : _____

2. Continue the skip-counting patterns.

a. 86, 76, 66, ________, ________, ________, ________, ________

b. 89, 91, 93, ________, ________, ________, ________, ________

3. Mom baked 30 peanut butter cookies and 25 chocolate chip cookies.

a. How many more peanut butter cookies than chocolate chip cookies did she bake?

b. How many cookies did she bake in total?

4. First subtract to 10. Then subtract the rest.

a. 17 − 9 / \\ 17 − ____ − ____ = _____	**b.** 14 − 6 / \\ 14 − ____ − ____ = _____	**c.** 11 − 7 / \\ 11 − ____ − ____ = _____

5. Write the previous and next whole ten.

a. ______, 32 , ______	**b.** ______, 95 , ______	**c.** ______, 107 , ______

Skills Review 64

1. Put the events in order.
   Mark 1, 2, and 3.

Mom says "yes"!

Tim takes good care of "Skippy".

Tim asks Mom if he can have a dog.

2. Add or subtract.

a.

	tens	ones
	7	6
+	3	0

b.

	tens	ones
	9	9
−	5	8

c.

	tens	ones
	8	7
−	4	5

d.

	tens	ones
	6	7
+	2	2

3. Match.

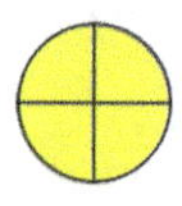

three quarters

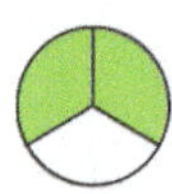

two halves

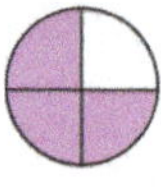

four fourths

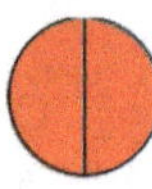

two thirds

4. Write the name of the month that goes in between.

a. September ____________________ November

b. February ____________________ April

c. July ____________________ September

Skills Review 65

1. The pictograph shows how many stuffed animals each girl has. **Each stuffed animal** picture means **4 stuffed animals**. One half of a stuffed animal would be half that.

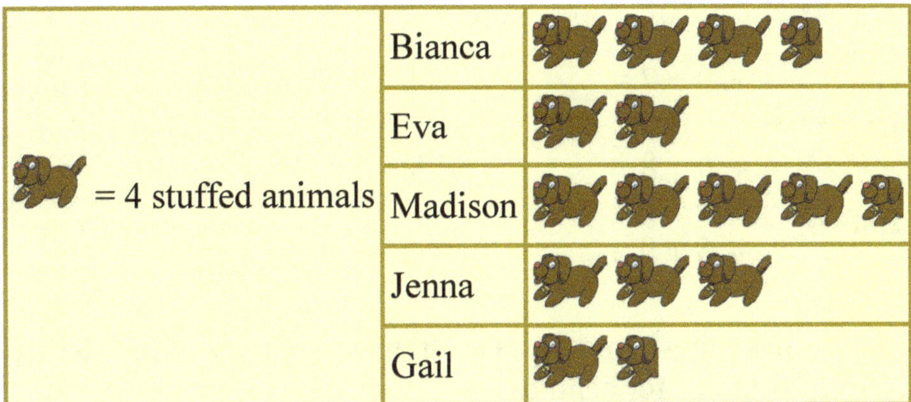

a. Who has the fewest stuffed animals? ________________________

How many stuffed animals does she have? _______

b. How many stuffed animals do Bianca and Gail have in total? _______

c. How many more stuffed animals does Madison have than Eva? _______

2. Count the dimes and nickels. Write the total amount in cents.

a. _______¢	**b.**  _______¢

3. Write the missing numbers.

a. _____ − 40 = 60	**b.** 10 + 30 + 50 = _____	**c.** 70 + _____ = 90
d. _____ + 20 = 100	**e.** _____ − 20 − 20 = 40	**f.** 60 − _____ = 30

4. Circle the event that takes a longer time.

a. Make a birthday card. Build a birdhouse.	**b.** Climb a ladder. Go down a slide.

Skills Review 66

1. Add. Tell which idea you use to add.

Trick with nine	a. 6 + 6 = _______	b. 8 + 7 = _______	Doubles chart
Trick with eight	c. 9 + 7 = _______	d. 8 + 8 = _______	"Just one more" than a double
"Just one more" than a sum with 10	e. 6 + 8 = _______	f. 6 + 5 = _______	
	g. 5 + 9 = _______	h. 7 + 4 = _______	I just know it!

2. Use real money to make these amounts. Or, draw gray circles with "10" for dimes, and orange circles with "1" for pennies.

a. 39¢	**b.** 12¢

3. Write < , > or = .

a. 9 + 9 ☐ 20 – 0 **b.** 50 + 20 ☐ 40 + 30 **c.** 48 – 3 ☐ 40 + 4

d. 76 – 3 ☐ 79 – 6 **e.** 62 + 5 ☐ 64 + 2 **f.** 39 – 5 ☐ 32 + 5

4. Solve the word problems.

a. Laura had 38 cents. Then, she lost 6 cents.
How much money does Laura have now?

Later, Laura's mom gave her 20 cents.
How much money does Laura have now?

b. Eric started cleaning his room at 2:30 and worked for two hours.
What time did he finish?

Half an hour later, Eric ate supper. What time was it?

Skills Review 67

1. Write the time using the expressions *o'clock* or *half past.*

a. ________________ ________________

b. ________________ ________________

c. ________________ ________________

d. ________________ ________________

2. Carol read 20 pages in a book. Later she read 10 more pages.

   a. How many pages did she read in total?

   b. If the book is 50 pages long, how many pages does she have left to read?

3. Write a fact family to match the picture.

____ + ____ = ____   ____ – ____ = ____

____ + ____ = ____   ____ – ____ = ____

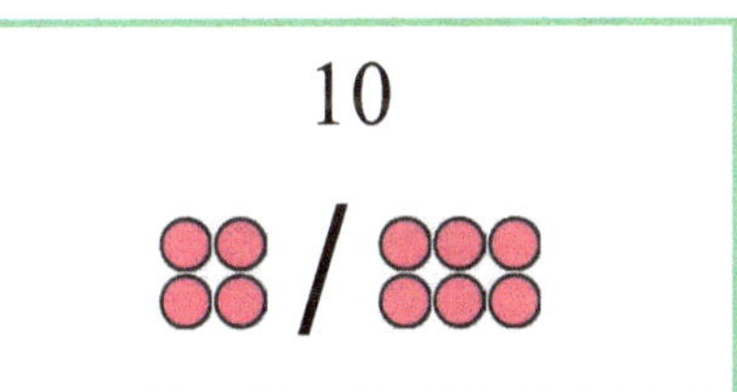

4. Right or not? Correct the additions that are *false* (wrong).

a. $9 + 8 = 16$ **b.** $8 + 4 = 12$ **c.** $5 + 9 = 14$ **d.** $8 + 6 = 15$

5. Write the total amount in cents.

a. 

b. 

c. 

Skills Review 68

1. The pictograph shows how many loaves of bread Sweety's Bakery sold during five days. Each picture of a loaf of bread represents 6 loaves of bread. A picture of half of a loaf of bread would represent 3 loaves of bread.

a. On what day did the bakery sell the most loaves of bread? ____________________

b. How many more loaves of bread were sold on Tuesday than on Thursday? ________

c. How many loaves of bread were sold on Monday and Wednesday, in total? ________

2. Cross out the coins you need to buy the item. Write how many cents you have left.

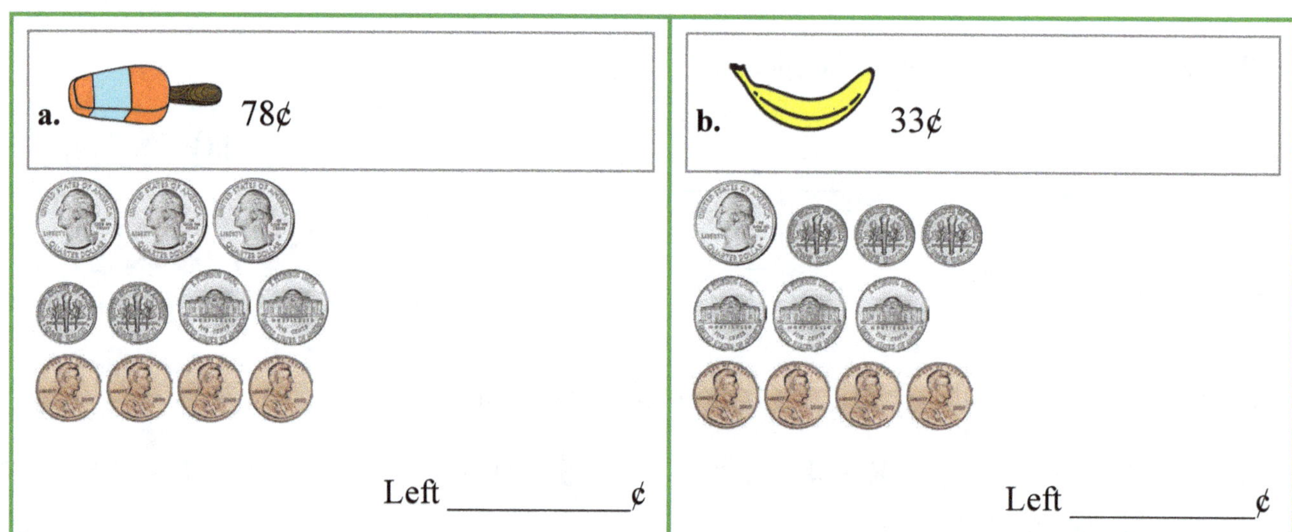

3. Continue the skip-counting patterns.

a. 99, 101, ______, ______, ______, ______, ______, ______

b. 120, 115, ______, ______, ______, ______, ______, ______

Skills Review 69

1. Kathy asked some people what animal they liked best. Draw bars for the bar graph.

Cat	15
Dog	18
Horse	9
Rabbit	6

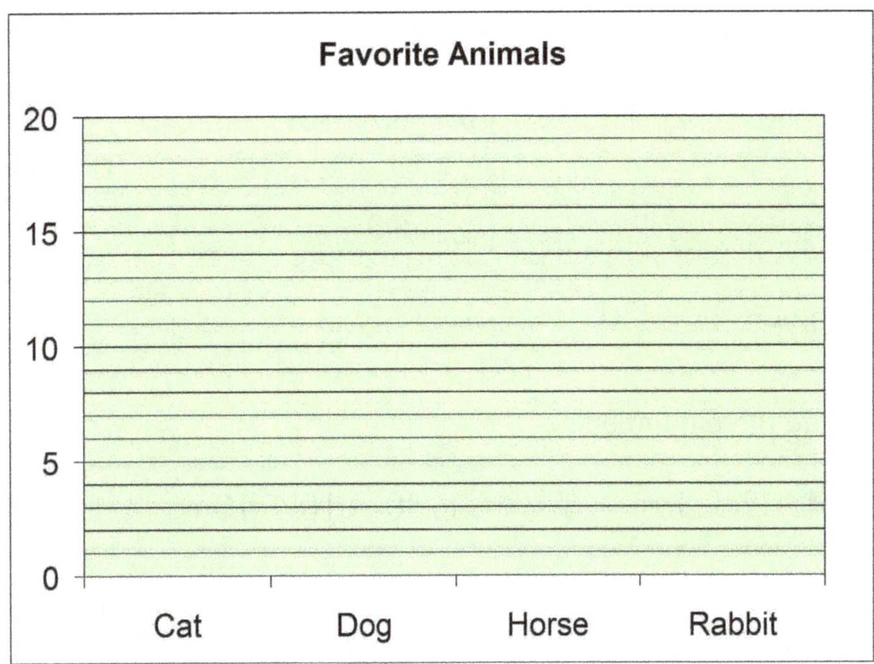

a. How many people liked horses and rabbits best, in total? ____________

b. Make one more question about this bar graph and tell it to your teacher.

2. Name the shapes. Then measure their sides and write their lengths.

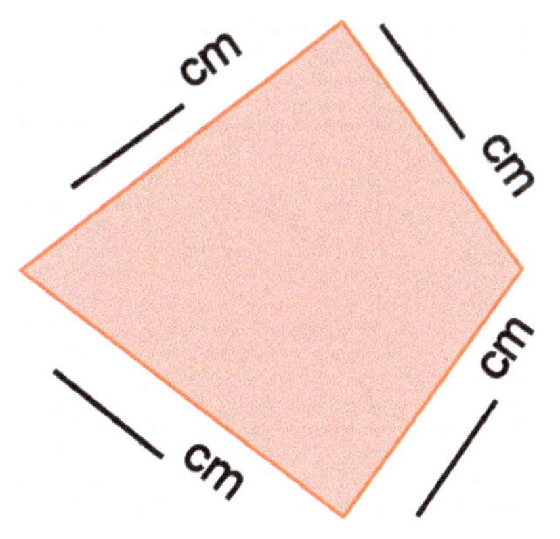

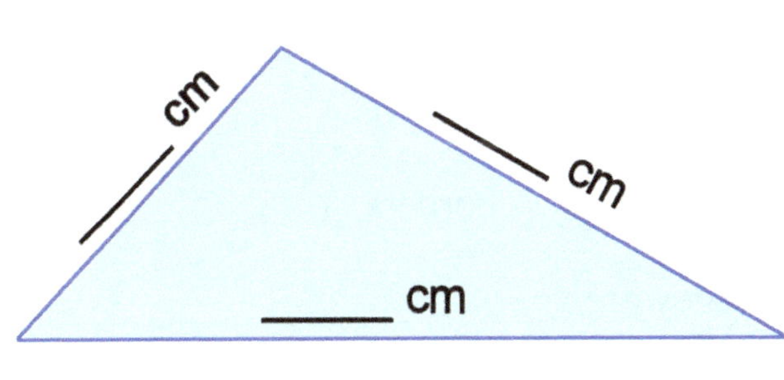

a. ________________________________ b. ________________________________

3. Megan wants to buy a pen that costs 89¢. She has 63¢. How much more money does she need?	4. Megan decides to buy some stickers for 10¢ each instead. How many can she buy with her 63¢? How much money will she have left?

Skills Review 70

1. Split the second number into two parts so that you can complete the next ten.

a. 66 + 7	**b.** 85 + 6	**c.** 27 + 9
/ \	/ \	/ \
66 + ____ + ____	85 + ____ + ____	27 + ____ + ____
70 + ____ = ______	______ + ____ = ______	______ + ____ = ______

2. Add three numbers.

a. 4 + 2 + 3 = ________	**b.** 30 + 10 + 10 = ________	**c.** 10 + 7 + 2 = ________

3. Draw a line from dot to dot so that you divide the shape into two new shapes. Use a ruler. How many sides do the new shapes have? How many corners?

a. The new shapes have _______ sides,

and _______ corners.

They are ___________________________

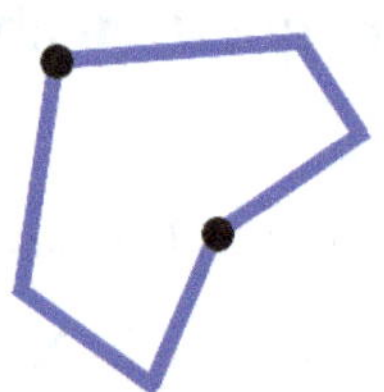

b. The new shapes have _______ sides,

and _______ corners.

They are ___________________________

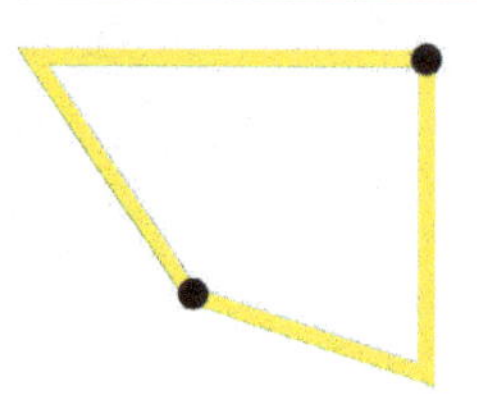

4. How much is the total if you have:

a. three dimes, a quarter, and a nickel

b. three quarters, one dime, and five pennies

5. Subtract.

a.	**b.**	**c.**	**d.**
99 – 5 = _____	56 – 4 = _____	18 – 3 = _____	37 – 7 = _____

2
2
3
4
4
5
5
5
5
1
1
1
1
1
1
3
4
6
7
4
7
6

This page intentionally left blank.

www.ingramcontent.com/pod-product-compliance
Lightning Source LLC
LaVergne TN
LVHW061339060426
835511LV00014B/2020
* 9 7 8 1 9 4 2 7 1 5 3 3 7 *